SOLITAIRE

[an affair with my heART]

BARBARA HARKNESS

BOOK TWO

PUBLISHED BY

Life is ART

www.barbaraharkness.com

Cover design and text layout © designed by Barbara Harkness

Published by Life IS Art Publishing
First published as (an affair with my heART) 2021
Second edition 2022

ISBN: 978-0-6456712-0-9 (print)
ISBN: 978-0-6456712-1-6 (ebook)

This book is dedicated to
Robert, Daniel and Max Harkness

CONTENTS

PART 1 - ART IMITATING LIFE

PART 2 - LIFE IMITATING ART

"There are a tremendous number of people suffering from an intention deficit disorder. They have no intention, they have no purpose, they have no mission and they're just living life reacting to circumstances and situations. To come to the world and to leave the world the same as when you arrived here means you didn't live your purpose. You didn't give your gift, you didn't share your passion. You are here on purpose, you are made from purpose."

- Michael Beckwith

PART 1

ART IMITATING LIFE

Prologue

It's a game, this privileged thing called life! A stage upon which we enact our finely crafted lines with other players - or is it all improvisation, making it up as we go along? The long game, the end game, games within games. Playing different roles and adjusting to the characters we are assigned along the journey. Then quite suddenly the end-game seems near, and you think *'well that was quick, have I really lived my best life?'* According to Socrates "The unexamined life is not worth living!" Which was how I came to find myself at the mid century mark, and by examining my existence gave myself a great big *audit* of the heart. I chose to play the game of Solitaire - to have an affair with my own heart and indulge in the solitude and patience required for the *'art'* to appear.

This story is that journey, from yet another *'death'* within a lifetime, to the *'re-birth'* of my true nature as an artist (at such a late stage in my life I might add). Better late than never as one would say! I reflect on my seventeen-year-old self, gazing out the window at work and thinking to myself *'it's just not happening here, so I'd better go and find it'* - my life! I resigned that afternoon from my job, went home to my parents and gave notice to my childhood as well. Within a fortnight I had left Wellington, New Zealand and my adolescence behind, boarded a plane for Sydney Australia and welcomed womanhood in an exciting new city where no one knew me. It was a brave decision, yes, but I was bold and confident and full of hope for my future (not that I had much of a plan back then). I was only seventeen and happy to have an adventure, which is my life - the life I have made for myself as a result of that brave decision. I was also being true to my nature, as my journey had begun.

Changing direction in life is rarely easy; this I know, as it took several years to redirect my ship when I got the call at age fifty-five to change it up, because it was *'time'* - again! I needed to simplify, to unravel the tightly knit jumper I was wearing and lead a lifestyle free of conformity and others' ideals. Moreover I wanted to be just me again.

Making the change we desire can require enormous fortitude to stay on track. Changing the environment or a job helps: that is the physical aspect. But it is the inner personal work needed to accompany the physical shift to walk a new path that truly challenges us to move out of our comfort zone. To get back onto my creative path as an artist, I changed my environment by selling the marital home and moving into my former home, a house I had always loved which had become my investment property upon marrying for a second time. I relished the idea of making it my own home again, a place just for me, and I am reminded of the writings by Virginia Woolf in *'A Room of One's Own'*. These days a woman needs a backup plan, and *'A House of One's Own!'*

My design company of twenty years had been a great success, with my notorious wine label design [Yellowtail] achieving superstar status as an international phenomenon. Nothing more to prove to myself (or anyone else) that I could create and run a business, therefore I gave notice (to the business-model me), and handed my design company over to my son, allowing the new guard to take over. Addressing my emotional and mental health, I dissolved my marriage of ten years to my second husband, knowing that the relationship had simply run its course.

I was to spend the next five years at art school, in an effort to re-establish my craft by being around creative people and to achieve a piece of paper that stated I had a Bachelor of Fine Art. This was just the vehicle - the process of intention that steered the mother ship in a new direction. But finally jumping into the life raft took another five years to arrive at a point where I felt I had finally come home to myself again, as an artist.

This is my story, a memoir of a ten-year period of mostly solitary undertakings in my life when I let my soul guide me every step of the way. I was led back home, to my gift and art practice, which became a highly introspective personal journey taken through the visual language of surrealism and catharsis of story telling. These short stories can be read in any order, because there is no beginning, nor an end, there is only now. Please enjoy!

Chapter 1

I had a dream, the wakeup call

"A dream is a small hidden door
in the deepest and most intimate sanctum of the soul,
which opens up to that primeval cosmic night that was
the soul, long before there was the conscious ego."

\- Carl Jung

I wake from a dream, turn to my husband and announce, "I don't want to be married anymore". The words spill out immediately upon waking, without any consideration of the consequences. The dream had exposed my current reality. I no longer recognized my husband. We were different people to when we'd married ten years prior and were now simply going through the motions of a conventional marriage. The dream had become my awakening.

I am in a wide corridor, the walls and floor are made from large sandstone blocks, the roof is high and arched, the building is medieval. I am observing myself from behind, as I glide precariously through the corridor. I am wearing a beautiful bright red silk dress with a long train, which flows behind me. I am the witness, observing. Where am I? What's going on? What's happening? I can sense this is an important day. I want in, - and so I slip into my body to feel the moment and understand what is happening. Aha - this is my wedding day! I now walk rather than glide, tentatively through the long corridor. A soprano begins to sing Ave Maria and I start to cry. Am I happy or sad? I don't know. I am simply filled with raw emotion spilling out of me through my tears. The corridor leads to a quadrangle, and I finally recognize the place. It is the Cathedral of San Lorenzo in Florence, where my husband and I had sat on the wall beneath the arches on our honeymoon in 2001. We'd taken photographs together there. In the centre of the quadrangle is a group of strangers, carefully watching my every move, my every reaction (just as his family did on our wedding day). The groom is in the middle, dressed in a smart black suit, his back is to me and he does not turn around. What am I doing here? I don't know any of these people, and I don't even know who the man is that I am marrying? Yet I am curious to know. Quietly I weep, and I still don't know how to feel. This is my wedding day, so surely they are tears of joy? But no, - I decide that they are tears of sorrow.

When I cannot walk any further, I am at the group, standing directly behind the groom. All eyes are upon me now. The groom finally turns around - he is not my husband! Standing before me is a total stranger - shorter, thick-set, and bearded. The complete opposite of my husband, and I don't recognize this man at all.

Rewind thirteen years: We are in a Bar, "Bin 273", sipping wine, and I am admiring my beautiful Italian boyfriend of three whole months. The candlelight enhances and charges the atmosphere with love vibes.

He gazes back, we are locked in a state of euphoric consensus.

"If I asked you to marry me, would you say yes?"

"Is that a question, or a proposal?" I reply.

"Well, would you marry me? I guess it is a proposal."

In the mood of the seductive moment, I said "yes." But in the cold hard light of the next day I called and said "no". Candles have a lot to answer for! I was not sure I ever wanted to marry again. I'd only known him for three months, and whilst we had confessed to each other we were in love, marriage felt wrong for me, outdated. I had my own home, my independence and was fully committed to my career. I had to be, I ran my own business and had employees to manage. Of course, there was time for a personal relationship and don't get me wrong, I wanted one. But marriage? Not sure it was my bag anymore, or even necessary.

"How about a relationship contract?" I countered. The idea of a renewable commitment contract based on mutual consensus, where relationship issues are addressed rather than ignored, (or worse still, stacked onto the pile of regrets that fester into resentment). This seemed far more practical. Renewable on negotiable five, seven or ten-year terms, which addressed the aspects of lifestyle, assets, extended family, habits, health and apathy. Everything should be on the table for assessment because let's face it, as we age, things change! Our bodies, attitudes, fortunes, health, even our extended families (and trust me these can be a major factor of dissent in second-time-around relationships) all morph with the passage of time. Who in their right mind would risk their lifetime accumulative assets to put them on the line, only to start again? But we see it happen time and time again through marriage failures. I think (and these are my own personal views) that in this modern age, which offers so much choice, it's crazy to limit our ideals within the old-fashioned rules and regulations the institution of marriage offers.

I was not against the whole idea of committing to building a life with someone, but I could sense a certain pattern happening once more. My first husband had also asked me at the three-month mark to marry him. Ironically I had also met him at a bar (as you did back then). Was there a certain blueprint that re-occurred when romantic love showed up? Or was I just being offered the same scenario to fix. Like a groundhog day, but with marriage of course it goes on for years, and years and years, until you wake up! Marriage may have suited me for twenty years in my first marriage, for all the things it was designed for: to provide a secure environment to bring children into the world. But did it necessarily suit me the second time around? That's a great big NOOOO, from me (with the benefit of hindsight). I was applying an old formula, when in fact I needed to move to a new level of existing and co-habiting. I felt that I had *grown out* of marriage because it simply did not suit my new way of being. In defence of my stupidity at repeating the same mistake, I was only eighteen years old when I first married. I was forty when I encountered the same scenario again and I should have known better, especially because I knew myself by then. Well, I thought I did!

I didn't want to be owned again. I didn't need to take anyone else's name. I had a perfectly good name, which I used in my business. It was the same name as my two sons', so why would I want to renounce that?

I managed to postpone co-habiting for two years by stating that a suitable courtship period strengthens a relationship. But sometimes I just needed him to leave, because I wanted my space and I was acutely aware of this. The separate house thing worked well for me so I really can't explain how I let this rather surprising act happen, but it did. I felt as though I'd been badgered into the next phase of our relationship because right on the two-year mark, I was pressured into 'living together'!

I purchased a rather large home where we could combine our Brady Bunch of four. As we both had two teenage children each, a four bedroomed house complete with a swimming pool seemed like a perfectly good idea at the time! Perhaps it was my need for more *space,* as the relationship happened predominantly at my house. Now teenage children don't ask to be a part of their parents failed marriages nor necessarily want to be a part of their parent's romantic ambitions with a new partner. Well mine didn't and neither did his, so we found out after the fact. Therefore we set about doing what most couples do (because the children were never there), we renovated the new home.

The first year I remember well and with fondness, possibly because we weren't married and genuinely did want our commitment to each other to work. The home was amazing. I had found it quite by accident, which had naturally precipitated the move and how we found ourselves playing house together. It was an Italian style villa modelled from a house in Tuscany, which had inspired the original owners to replicate. It was an authentic Italian style home with large porticos, pink rendered walls, Italian tiles, and backed onto a reserve that had a plantation of majestic two-hundred-year-old red river gums with a creek running through it. The trees were a haven for birdlife so the days were filled with the most gorgeous sounds of nature, and when it rained the creek flowed and could also be heard from the house. Sometimes this became a torrent, depending on the rainfall. It was a large home built in the mid-seventies with a lot of the original décor still intact, right down to the shag pile carpet, mirrored fireplaces, and dated Italian tiles, which of course meant a total overhaul was necessary to make it palatable to our tastes. For me, it became a design project, which allowed for my creative interior designer to flourish!

The new home was also good for my beautiful Italian partner, as there were wild olive trees in the reserve at the back of the property, which he picked and cultivated yearly, and gradually mastered the art of bottling olives. Each year the olives were perfected as the trees responded to their yearly cull, and his recipes improved through the experimentation process. He was a domestic god in the kitchen and around the house for that matter. He vacuumed, he ironed, he dusted, and he cooked. He was meticulously tidy, fully functional in the bedroom, life was good, - it didn't get much better than this. Utopia!

Now when I travelled for business, (and as most do) I would tack on a little holiday sojourn at the end of the trips. When we decided to do *Vinitaly* (an annual international wine and spirits exposition) a year or so into our co-habiting, he suggested going to visit his family in the Veneto region. He had a large family of uncles, aunts and cousins. Even his ninety-four-year-old grandmother was still alive. Before we left, he suggested that we *tie the knot* elopement style whilst we were over there. I still didn't see the point, and would have rather lived with the insecurity of *whatever will be, will be*. However, I also convincingly managed to argue the point with myself; he was tall, dark, handsome, domestically trained, helpful, encouraging, culinarily creative, intelligent, sex was good and I loved him. So why not marry the guy? We were living as man and wife anyway, and so far so good, so maybe we should take that next step? *'Faciamo el paso'*, is what he would say to me when we did argue, *'move on, and move past it to the next'*. And the *next* for us was marriage. It meant a lot to him, his Italian values. He wanted me to be his wife, and so I agreed.

We set about acquiring all the documentation required for a registry wedding in Italy somewhere, place unknown at this point. We would work that out when we got there. Divorce decrees, birth certificates, nationality papers, passports, all had to be translated into Italian before we left. I didn't buy a dress because we were going to orchestrate it all when we got there, and only *if* we could pull it off that is. He wanted to buy me the dress and I wanted to wear red. This was my only requirement if I had to do this thing, I didn't want a white wedding! I wanted to be a scarlet woman of passion!

Now pulling off an elopement in Italy is no mean feat. All the documents needed to first be acknowledged by the Australian Consulate;

stamped and issued with a marriage licence. The consulate was in Milan, which constituted a day trip by train, presenting our documents, yet not knowing if we would receive them back at all that day, nor even during the time of the vacation. This was our first step into this venture, but I would have been equally content if the paperwork did not eventuate. We wrote our vows over lunch on the back of a paper napkin, the day we took the documents to Milan. They suited our idea of flexibility, within the constraints of the ideals of what marriage meant to us both. I was caught up in the flow now, but this was not my flow, it was his.

'I do promise to honour, cherish and respect you, through love, trust and understanding. I will be your lover and your friend. I will be your strength and your comfort in times of need. I will stand by you and face our life together, with all the joys and sorrows that may occur. I will respect your individuality, and I will nurture our growth in this union together. I give you my heart, body and soul to share. These promises I make to you in this lifetime.'

Yeah, that sounded pretty flexible, a contract with just a hint of romanticism. When we arrived back from Milan that evening we presented the marriage license to his uncle, who rubbed his hands together in glee and proclaimed, *"abbiamo un matrimonio, cominciamo - we have a wedding, let's get started!"* He engaged his next-door neighbour who was the local retired Commissioner of Police to open all the necessary doors for us to get the documents stamped. It was crazy. We drove to Padua, and then Verona to have the documents stamped time and time again, the same procedure and every time with Euros exchanged. The fee was usually unknown, so to me, it seemed like a little racket of making sure your mates were all looked after.

Then there was the interview with the Lord Mayor of Castle

Franco herself, to make sure that we were serious about what we were embarking on. This was the location we had chosen for the wedding as our original thoughts of a Venice wedding got canned when we found out there was a $6,000 contribution to the Restoration of Venice fund. Which was fine for movie stars who could afford it. As I could not speak Italian, for legal reasons, we needed a translator for the initial interview (which was more like a police interrogation) and for the wedding also. The translator turned out to be from Adelaide. She was the daughter of friends of his parents. The village indeed, the Italian village was even smaller, but widely spread throughout the world. During the *interrogation,* I was asked many questions. Note: this wasn't like going to the local priest for a few tips on the conjugal duties and responsibilities of a husband and wife.

"Have I ever been convicted of murder?"

"No, I got away with it."

"Am I carrying another man's child?"

"I'm not sure, I think he used a condom."

At which point I laughed out loud and said, *"of course I'm not"*, but they continued with the archaic process of medieval interrogation. It did not go down well and I was told off and reprimanded over my frivolity because marriage was a serious affair and it appeared that I was not taking it seriously! Of course, of course! But the doubt had started to creep in at that point. The interrogation hit a nerve somehow, yes this was a very serious thing I was doing. Did I *really* want to do this?

I was swept away by it all. I went with the flow and said yes to everything. His family all pitched in and organised the details; from photographer to rings, hair styling to the bouquet, morning tea and drinks, all of it was arranged through the generosity of the family. My lack of the local lingo I shall admit, contributed to this, however. a huge part of me was detached from it all. Subconsciously I was happy to *not* partake in the details, and considering my position on marriage, it suited me just fine. We never found a red dress, even though we searched the alleyways and boutiques of Venice to the point of exhaustion. Settling for a nice cream Giorgio Armani ensemble in the end and from desperation on the day before the main event. It was appropriately matrimonial. I simply frocked up and rocked up on the day. His Uncle drove me to the town hall of the moat-surrounded township of Castle Franco for the eleven o'clock wedding to my Italian partner of three years. We had not seen each other since the previous day and he was waiting for me at the venue upstairs in the elaborate proceedings room, along with twenty-five of his relatives. The lord Mayoress wore a red, white and green sash across her torso like a beauty queen. We made our vows, Ave Maria played, it was beautiful and everyone cried - except me!

After the ceremony, we walked the cobblestone streets along with an entourage of cousins and a photographer who captured and cheered our every embrace, every kiss, and every laugh. Yes, it was a happy and joyous event. We commandeered a small café for photos, coffee and pastries, whilst everyone stood at the bar admiring the recently wed couple. Later that evening as I lay in bed with my beautiful Italian husband, who was now peacefully asleep, reality struck and I thought quietly to myself, *OMG what have I done!* I had made my bed, and therefore my choice to lay in it, - for ten more years. They weren't bad years, but marriage changed everything, well for me it did. Evidently for him as well; he'd gotten the contract, I was now his wife and he felt secure enough to take his foot off the gas, after which we slowly glided downhill and ground to an eventual halt!

Ten years on, my marriage to this beautiful Italian man had become my worst nightmare, and what I feared, had manifested into a self-fulfilling prophecy. Perhaps it is not that we cannot be who we want to be in marriage; it is simply that the expectations we put on ourselves, and our partner don't allow for the time to dedicate to our own development.

I had often heard it said that if you marry an Italian man you take on the role of their mother as well. Was this also what was expected of me? I began to feel uneasy, questioning, I knew if this was an expectation, then I could not fulfil it. The trade-off instead was that I became the social secretariat in the marriage, for my sanity more so. I was never sure his mother had wanted us to marry, possibly because I was not Italian. Over the years the weight of that, real or imagined, produced a feeling in me that I could not do anything right in her eyes.

I still loved my husband but was questioning my lifestyle and the role that seemed to have been carefully carved out for me. I knew that if I stayed I would be unhappy with the rest of my life. I had spent the past eleven years trying to be the perfect partner to my husband, doing it all by the book, (NOT the Italian version, however) and fulfilling the expectation we had created when we first fell in love. But people change, they quite often *grow into each other*, and maybe this is a sign of a successful marriage. Conversely, you can also *grow out of each other.*

In life, without ideas, there can be no progress, and in the long run, survival depends upon creativity which requires risk, and living with the energy of inventive ideas and creating new ways of living through sheer imagination. I was feeling stifled and blocked. I knew there was a much better way of living. When we are ready, the Universe has ways of providing a path to us. We simply need to see the signs along the way, or ignore them at our peril!

I have often likened life to a vessel, in particular a boat. We start off as children, sailing in dinghies with one sail. We don't venture far from shore and are happy to let the wind and the current take us where we need to go. Along life's path, we often trade up to a larger vessel. I had in this instance, found myself in a Gondolier being swooned and cajoled down the narrow waterways, which eventually led to one of those Ocean liners. Yes, the ones whose propellers are damaging the pillars Venice is built upon. Well, I am not so sure that the foundations for our marriage were that solid to begin with. But the Titanic we had found ourselves on seemed doomed to hit an iceberg eventually and I knew it. Rather than go down with a sinking ship I decided to turn the engines off. One by one I shut them down. However, a ship takes a long time to grind to a halt, especially a large one with people on board. I made sure all the people got off safely (my employees). I let them voluntarily disembark for fairer shores, but never replaced the crew. I wound my business down to a point where it was being kept alive on life support with just one engine burning – me!

This was a powerful validation to myself of how, when you divert energy away from something, it dies. This can occur in so many facets; family, marriage, work, business, friendships. Everything in life takes a concerted amount of effort and energy. It was at this point when the last engine had been switched off and it was gliding to its halt, that I decided to *jump ship*. I managed to land softly on a much smaller one. I am repairing the years of neglect it has endured, but I shall make it beautiful again. More importantly, I am the skipper of my own vessel; there is no team required to run it, and no ship's mate either. Had I stayed on the Titanic, I had the foresight to know it was going to go down.

And that knowledge was through the pattern of experience. Hindsight, they say is a wonderful thing, but foresight is the use of this intuitive quality we all possess which annuls hindsight (if we choose to use it). It has been said that every battle is won before it is fought. Well, I certainly chose to fight my battle before the bun-fight began. I knew I needed to reclaim my life. I had given it my best shot. So powerful was the dream, that I could not ignore the fact that my soul was guiding me via my very personal movie, shown in vivid technicolour, complete with a blatantly obvious script to follow.

We agreed to go our separate ways but still lived in the same house for economic reasons. This was very difficult, to say the least. The push and pull of a relationship in the death throws where two people still care for each other was confusing for us both. My resolve was questioned often; I am after all, only human! When two dear friends suggested we travel to Italy with them for a special birthday, we agreed, in an attempt to resurrect the marriage. It was a very spur of the moment decision, and one I secretly wished I had not agreed to. But this is what we do isn't it? We try to make marriages work because we don't like the idea of failure. I certainly didn't relish being a second time offender in the marriage stakes. But I had hoped that the trip to Italy might spur some decision-making on my husband's part. After all, it was where we had married ten years ago, and it was his homeland. He spoke fluent Italian so it was easy for him. He became more attractive in Italy, that was a given. But I needed him to plan, to be excited by, and to pay for the trip. I'd done enough, way too much in facilitating our lifestyle, and was tired of doing it all. These were my self-imposed expectations, I know. Had he stepped up and delivered, perhaps we may have gone on for a few more years, but in my heart of hearts I knew we were applying a band-aid. As a result of his apathy, I suggested that he didn't come to Italy with me, two weeks before we were due to leave.

"I want to go with just my friends instead."

He looked at me and cried. He knew that this was the last opportunity to fix our marriage. By this stage I was beyond the point of no return, I guess. I wanted to go to Venice with my friends, and then on to London to meet my half-sister for the first time and say goodbye to another friend who had only months to live. My agenda had changed and I simply didn't want to do any of it with him. I was taking a stance and trusting my gut instinct.

So off to Venice I ventured with my friend of twenty-five years and her husband. I was staying in a hotel and my friends were staying at a bed and breakfast on the Lido. We would ferry into Venice daily. There was one particular day that struck me with signs. You know, how sometimes you just have days when you feel that someone from the celestial world is trying to tell you something? The first instance was at breakfast in the B&B with my friends and their hosts. I looked around the Cucina surroundings and came across a little plaque placed on a shelf. It read, *'Anything is possible.'* This was my husband's and my mantra together - from the early days, I might add. We did believe that we could do anything. In business, in marriage, it was all connected for us and we did kick some real goals in the early years, personally and professionally, together. For a moment - I missed him, but I wouldn't be human if I didn't have feelings of reflection, especially being in the country where we had married. I let the melancholy feeling sit with me, and then slide slowly away.

That same day we had a tour planned to visit the secret gardens of Venice with a personal guide. We met her at the wharf and she immediately proceeded to inform us about the city of Venice. Upon arrival into the city, there is a tower with a remarkable gold statue perched upon its pinnacle. I asked the guide about the origins of this statue and she remarked that it was the Chamber of Commerce, and the statue was Fortuna; a befitting figure, an angel with wings coated in pure gold leaf, shining like a beacon above the once powerful, financial maritime city of Venice.

Our guide informed me with just enough to whet my appetite for the Goddess Fortuna; who was the Roman counterpart of the Greek Goddess Tyche. During the early Renaissance era, a migration of Greek scholars (from the fall of Constantinople) brought with them texts and scriptures, which saw a resurgence of Greek philosophy and mythology (referred to as Greek Classicism in art terms). Their mythical stories of Gods and Goddesses gave reverence to the human and earthly existence and were used as inspiration for allegorical content during the Renaissance era. These scriptures helped birth the Renaissance, hence the adaption of the many Gods and Goddesses to suit their burgeoning cultural movement. I liked Tyche straight away, in fact, I identified with her. She is a little more mysterious than the Goddess Fortuna, whom the Italians had decided only bestowed *good luck* upon her patrons, hence her position atop the Chamber of Commerce. Tyche held a far more discriminatory view on how she bestowed *fate* and *fortune* to her followers. Tyche personified that peculiar combination of circumstances we call *'luck'*, but she also dealt out unexpected downfalls in fortune -*bad luck*! She is variously represented holding a rudder (for turning the ship either way) or a sceptre (her magic wand), but she always holds a cornucopia of gold coins. Sometimes she appears blindfolded, indicating the unknown aspect of how fate's hand will be dealt. She was often depicted as a figurehead on many warships, which went into battle, as they depended upon her favourability toward their reverence to her presence. Likewise, they could also blame her if she did not deliver a victorious outcome. Whilst Tyche is a Goddess who loves to weld her power in unpredictable ways, she teaches the paradoxical message that life is essentially a game of dice, determined by chance. No matter how submissive we are to fate, when undecided about life, Tyche actually encourages taking control of your direction and therefore your destiny is entirely up to you. The success of our ventures is never guaranteed, but there still needs to be the optimism of chance, which is when your destiny arrives, and (hopefully) your fortune along with it. Ultimately if the intention is honourable and pure, Tyche usually rewards your efforts. Adversely, men and women have fallen on their swords when Tyche, that harlot of ill fate, decides a lesson is far more valuable than a reward. She can pull that rug right out from under you as quickly as the magic carpet took you soaring to new heights. And this was how I discovered Tyche, the Goddess of *fate and fortune* - and my *go-to* Goddess, in times of need!

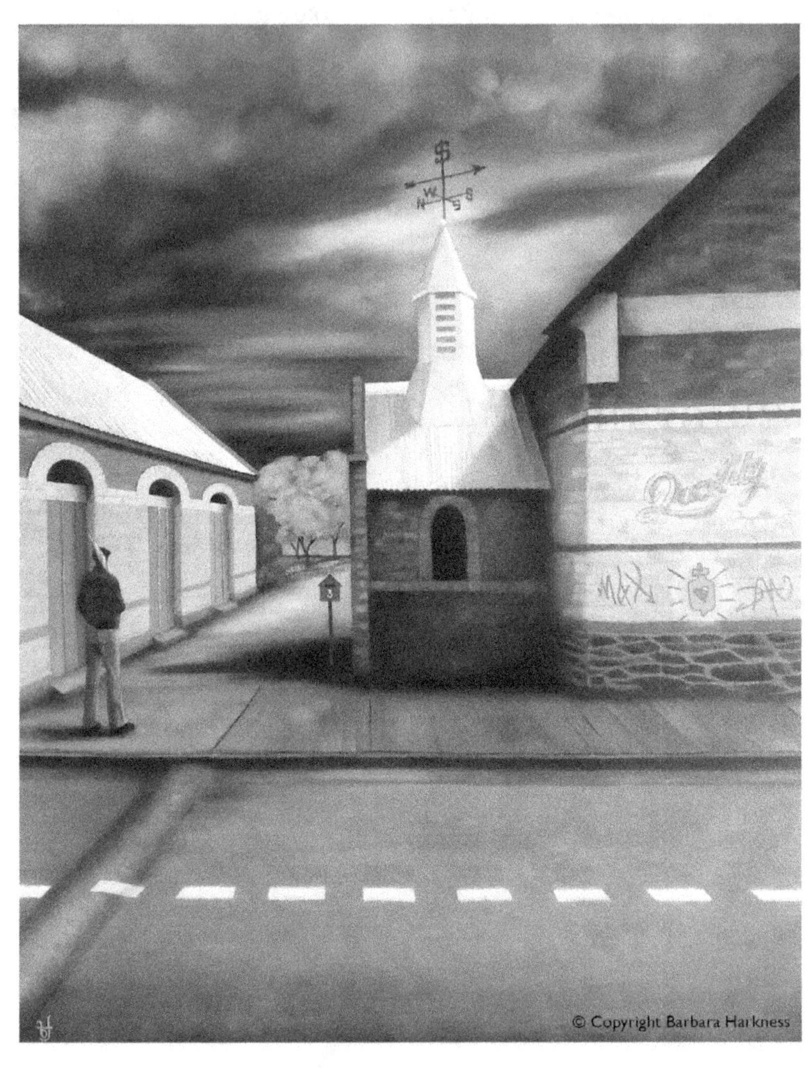

3 Mile End

Chapter 2

Deconstructing my perfectly designed life

"I think it is healthy to spend time alone.
You need to know how to be alone,
and not be defined by another person"
- Oscar Wilde

Whilst I pondered the use of the word *deconstruction,* I realized that I was doing this through my creative pursuits and examining my life from a subverted perspective, in an attempt to expose and therefore understand my resistance to conformed ideals. Deconstruction (in art terms) isn't about destroying - rather, it's about undermining ingrained assumptions to view things in a new light through the interpretation of literature.[1]

The physical worldly aspects and assets were easy to dismantle. I sold off furniture, gave clothes away, changed out my BMW X5 status symbol for a small car and seriously considered not owning a car at all. The process was instinctive and intuitive; I surrendered to the voice within and let it all go. From here on I wanted the last trimester of my life to take on relevance and meaning in an authentic way. I no longer wanted the trappings of marriage or the material possessions of status. I was, however, a slave to the ideology of society's trappings of marriage, and to any outsider looking in, we appeared to have it all. After ten years together, we'd ended up with a magnificent million-dollar-plus home complete with an Audi (his) and BMW (mine) in the garage. It all looked pretty sweet from the outside; in fact, we had a very nice life. We entertained often,

[1] To deconstruct means to unravel, disentangle, decipher, dissect, decode and dismantle through the interpretation of literature.

threw parties, and enjoyed everything the house had to offer, which we extended to our friends. I would often come back from holidays, lie by the pool exhausted and wonder why we ever left when we had our own sanctuary right here in Adelaide. The house was hard to let go of because it was the conduit in the marriage. However, I knew instinctively that it was time to disembark at this station, and say goodbye...

Dear House,

We have restored your beauty over the past ten years we have owned you. Inch by inch, scrubbing, stripping, moving and moulding we peeled back your layers, and gave you the facelift you so deserved. You had good bones to start with and now you are adorned with the original Mediterranean heritage you so deserved. You are a grand majestic lady of some thirty-six years - in your prime and your beauty certainly shows.

We have both laughed and cried tears of joy and pain in you. The memories etched deeply into your thick walls will remain as the ghosts of Casa Barzana.

How we have enjoyed the parties, the wake and the wedding, dinners with friends, and plunging into the welcome waters of the pool on hot summers days (and nights).

Your location is pure Utopia, the solace of the wind in the trees, bullfrogs in the creek, and the chattering lorikeets is pure balm to my soul.

And now our work is done, it is time to pass you on to new owners to enjoy the fruits of our labour. My pride and joy - you are a reward I have found difficult to let go of. So forgive me dear house, the heart knows no reason that reason does not know. It is simply time to move on, for things change within us and the comforts we hold so close and guarded become the very shackles we need to break free from, in order to grow again.

I have exploited you for sure, as every room tells a different story. They have been created as mood boards for my changing appetite for life. From the Feng Shui garden through to the Moroccan hub I find a sense of calm so soothing that I simply could have stayed forever, in the panacea that you are. But that is not living really, is it?

You have been my most permanent home and possession in my life so far, and it is this love and respect for you that has sustained my existence.

We had a pink Tuscan Villa, and we called you Casa Barzana; we have loved you so much, and now it is time to leave.

Barbara

Knowing that I should have had the marriage annulled when I realised my mistake on our wedding night, I simply had to take responsibility for *not* allowing it to continue, despite the beautiful home we had created. Honestly - the house renovations satisfied my creative desires, which had kept me there, entertaining and playing house. But the perfect designer disguise was fast becoming a dysfunctional existence as man and wife. Owing to my disinterest in our life once the renovations were complete, the interior *house of cards* came crashing down when my soul spoke so clearly to me in the dream, and I didn't hesitate in acknowledging the message *'I don't want to be married anymore.'* Perhaps our souls help us to recognise the truth, when we can't find our way in life, and present to us in our dreams a far clearer picture?

Our de-coupling (to use a modern term) turned out to be a

mutually propitious agreement, and he moved on pretty quickly. He had also married very young the first time around and had experienced only one relationship before marrying me. The times had certainly changed since then and owing to his attractive appearance, he became a highly sought after commodity on internet dating sites. So there was a never-ending smorgasboard of women to aid his own journey. He would share some of the more interesting stories of enlightening encounters in the dating game, so nonetheless, he enjoyed his newfound freedom and we remained friends. By cutting him loose I had set him free.

The painting *3 Mile End* depicts the time when we were separating, Mile End is a suburb in Adelaide, and this particular scene was referenced from a photograph I took on a day when my two sons were visiting. It was one of our last family group outings, he still liked to be involved. We'd walked the streets of this historic suburb photographing the dilapidated Edwardian houses, (since we are all keen photographers). The suburb was being upgraded with massive high-rise apartment buildings, which dwarfed the quaint little cottages, and would eventually run them out of town. We'd found a great little Mile End cafe where we sat and ate cinnamon sticky buns with coffee afterwards. It was one of those memorable days I won't forget (all well photographically documented), but quite possibly it was the delicious buns and coffee we remembered most, as the Mile End walk was requested often upon their subsequent visits. Alas, the café is no longer there.

Whilst I am a realist painter and usually use photographic references for my subject matter, the painting overtakes the photograph at some stage. There are staged aspects to this image so let me explain the allegorical content: the inclusion and use of the number 3 references the superstitious adage *'things always happen in 3s'* – and there were 3 aspects of my life I was in the process of deconstructing; my business, our marriage, and the home. In a spiritual sense 3 is the number associated with the Holy Trinity (Father, Son, Holy Spirit), also the beginning, middle, end, and the past, present, future. I placed a common letterbox with the number 3 upon it next to the entry of the church, which represents the home, large and imposing, my intention here is to indicate a reverence to the spiritual nature of marriage and family. There are 3 doors on the building to the left, and these symbolise the 3 properties I had at the time (coincidentally these were all pink rendered and Italian in style). The churches cross upon the weather cock is now a $ sign, a reference to my fortune heading south (I knew it would as a result of what we were doing), and on the foundation of the church (the home) are my children's graffiti tags with the word *'Quality'* above these - a direct reference to my feelings at the time. A storm brews above and my husband stands to look back over the path we have walked together, his umbrella cast over his shoulder, awaiting the rain and pondering the probable pending fallout of our decision to part. The pink tree in the background, where love once blossomed is now discarding the foliage to become bare once more. I stand observing the scene, whilst I create it, the white line delineating my boundary; the speed bump in the road is also a metaphorical *bump* upon life's route. This painting was the first one I made which directed me onto the path and search for spiritual meaning - through the use of my own personal symbology. The painting was a project from art school, so it's a little out of context in my storyline, however, it fits with the subject matter of this chapter.

When I started the divorce proceedings, I found there was no record of our marriage in Australia; therefore I wondered if it was even valid? Seems all the forms we had to sign in Italy were just a nice little racket after all, and no validation of the marriage papers were ever sent back to Australia (as promised by the authorities in Italy at the time). Not one to leave t's uncrossed or i's un-dotted, I proceeded with the Italian version of our marriage papers through the Australian courts and managed to get a piece of paper which stated *'Divorce Decree'* with both of our names underneath. I was happy with that. I guess I was a stickler for abiding by the rules when it came to securing my future and that of my children.

The business was quite possibly the easiest part of my life to dismantle simply by taking my focus and attention away from it. I love the saying *'where attention goes - energy flows'* and vice versa. When you take the attention away, the energy also stops flowing. As employees left for other jobs, I never replaced them, and I lived off the proceeds of designs, which were still in the market for sale. In 1999 my business was the total focus of my life, and I had the attitude of *'if it is to be - then it is up to me,'* and this personal philosophy helped me create a graphic design company that was responsible for one of the most famous wine labels ever launched [yellow tail]. However, I had never chosen to be a wine label designer – but this role defined my fate and served me very well financially for twenty years, and for that I am grateful. I think in hindsight, that creating a business was one of those things I wanted to try in life, and now it was time to do something else – just what, I wasn't yet sure of. As the company slowly wound down, I eventually relinquished my graphic design list of clients to my son and his new partner (who just happened to be a brilliant graphic designer). They changed the name owing to the fact they did not want to work in the same way I had. They wanted a London based model, which built brands on strategic brand analysis, a far more sophisticated concept. They have taken their new business to extreme heights I could never have imagined. When they did this, I knew that it was never my destiny, but theirs. Perhaps my place in the world with it was simply the germination of a business that would naturally evolve through the next generation. My son has made me proud in that arena - FYI: Co-Partnership.com

Chapter 3

The story of Piglet & Pooh

"What day is it Pooh?"
"It's today, Piglet."
"Oh good, that's my favourite day."
- A.A Milne

This is a story of the first friendship developed after I left the marriage. A case of *'be careful what you wish for!'* Wanted: a man with financial means, eastern suburbs preferred, well-educated, smart, must own his own home/s, business-minded, articulate, cultured. Damn, forgot to add good-looking - and young - well same age-ish!

My belief that we only know ourselves through relationship with others was being endorsed. Now that I did not have a *significant* other, I was free to express myself and discover who I really was without the constraints of *belonging* to someone else.

I met Rupert when I attended an art show with the added intention of wanting to meet someone new (besides viewing the art). What a great place to pick up indeed, at a well to do eastern suburbs prestigious yearly art show event, which is always well patronised by influential, well-to-do people with some degree of decorum. Until the alcohol kicks in, that is!

So, there I was pondering over a particularly lovely charcoal portrait of a young woman (which I ended up buying) when an older gentleman struck up an easy conversation with me about art. He called himself a collector; he simply loved buying paintings and small sculptural pieces for his three homes. A fact he dropped as the opener to our communication - a good choice of topic because, at the time, I also had three homes – snap, game on! We viewed the show together and by the end of the night, I had secured a lunch date for the following Sunday.

Now I have to confess that the dark shadows of night are kinder to us in our ageing years, aided by that great social lubricant - *alcohol,* or is this the time to point out that he was seventeen years my senior? Though there was a considerable age difference our conversation flowed and therefore, we enjoyed each other's company.

Rupert had lost his son twenty years ago and had not recovered from his loss. His son was a talented surgeon who had developed a brain tumour, which eventually claimed his life at age thirty-six. Rupert had been a business owner in the field of financial planning and insurance broking. He had built a successful business, which he sold, luckily just before the GFC. He had seen the writing on the wall well before it hit and escaped with his dosh and lifestyle intact. I found this aspect about him attractive, and along with his aesthetic for order and beautiful art meant we could converse on just about anything. He said he had never found a woman (that's me) with whom he could have these sorts of discussions. And this is where we connected. I was open to a friendship, however, after a second date I realised he was seeking more of a romantic relationship, but with our age difference, I wondered if it could work. I was living as a free spirit in my newly created Bohemian home, along with my own ideals.

Some eight months later, I broke and called him. I was bored! "Hey Rupert", I cut straight to the chase, "Want to take me out today? I've got cabin fever!"

However, those same previous feelings of despair upon his arrival still haunted me. He certainly had not grown any younger, none-the-less we developed a lovely friendship, which resulted in my endearingly calling him Pooh, and his response for me, - was Piglet.

On a deeper level, I knew that I was addressing something else. My first husband was twelve years my senior. At the age of sixteen I had even dated a man twenty years older than myself (yep, writing that feels weird and kind of sick I know, illegal even). I enjoyed his feelings of affection for me, and though I did not want to be his lover, his old-fashioned fatherly protection of me was endearing. Was I addressing the love I did not feel for my father by replacing it with the affection from an older man? Probably!

Now I do know that destiny does not take you where you don't want to go, so *love* never happened between us. Well for me it didn't. I think for Rupert it did. Aware as I was, that I did not want to hurt him, I still let the friendship roll itself out before me, and before I knew it, I was having an extraordinary *platonic* relationship. He adored me, and I needed to be admired and cherished. He took me away and bought me gifts. We would spend time visiting his hills property where he farmed cattle, or at his beach house, usually with lunch beforehand. He showered me with compliments, pampered me at spa retreats, and gorgeous hotels. And I was able to offer him equality at conversation, chess and billiards. We laughed constantly, and much of this laughter was the result of my quirks aimed at removing his crusty protective armour. Sometimes I thought I'd gone too far with my jibes, but he only laughed harder. I had become the muse!

I will never forget, however, when he divulged his despair at the end of his marriage and the loss of his children at that time. He cried like a child as I tucked him into bed, his body curled into the foetal position, his bald head poking out from the sheets, - the roles had reversed! But there is always this element of reciprocity in a relationship, isn't there?

I stroked his head gently, and said, "It's ok to cry, Rupert", but said silently to myself, *'it's not supposed to be like this, what have I done?'* He admitted that he often found himself in tears at the very thought of my calling and leaving a message and that I cared to call at all!

I needed so much more than being his confidant and muse. It was time! However, rather than even contemplate a relationship, it was now *time* to fully concentrate on me.

Chapter 4

Let's go to art school

"It had long since come to my attention
that people of accomplishment rarely sat back
and let things happen to them.
They went out and happened to things."

- Leonardo Da Vinci (artist, inventor, creator of things)

I had always liked Psychology; I was drawn to the great philosophers and had a certain fascination about mythology and the mystics. I knew that going to university would help steer my ship around, but was not sure which boat I wanted to board. I chose a degree in Fine Art over Psychology after much pondering, because I felt Psychology would have led to creating another business. And I did not want to do *business* anymore.

Art galleries were not only a source of inspiration for me, they also offered solace during this time of contemplation about my future. In 2012 a retrospective exhibition was being shown at the Art Gallery of South Australia by the local South Australian artist Anna Platten. From the moment I stepped into the gallery, I was riveted to the floor in awe. I had never seen such a complex narrative of art in my entire life. These masterfully executed allegorical works of art depicted her struggle with motherhood, sexuality, confinement, love; what it was to be a woman. Thirty years of her life displayed in one massive gallery was quite a sight to behold. I understood instantly the power of her personal investigation and how she had used her life experience for inspiration. A series of paintings I have chosen to use in my book depicts a woman riding a hobbyhorse. The character having woken from her dream embarks on an epic land journey that takes her across time and space. Inspired by

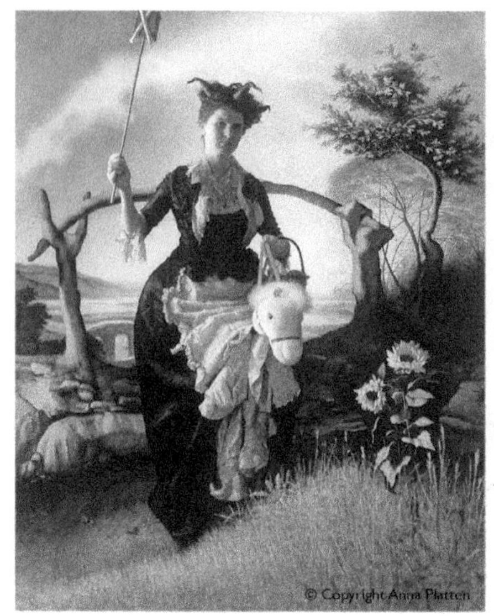

Landmark 2009

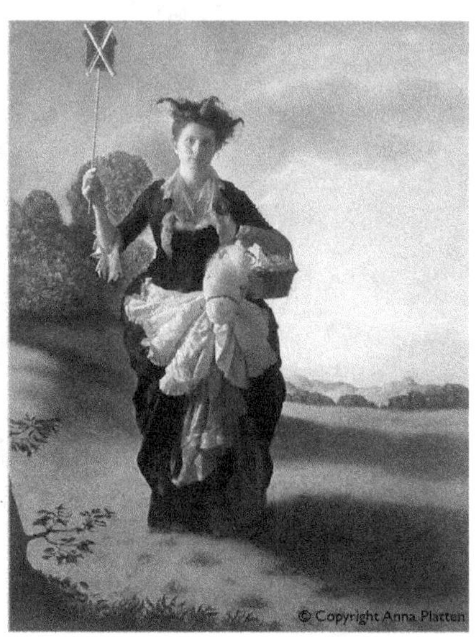

The Journey 2008

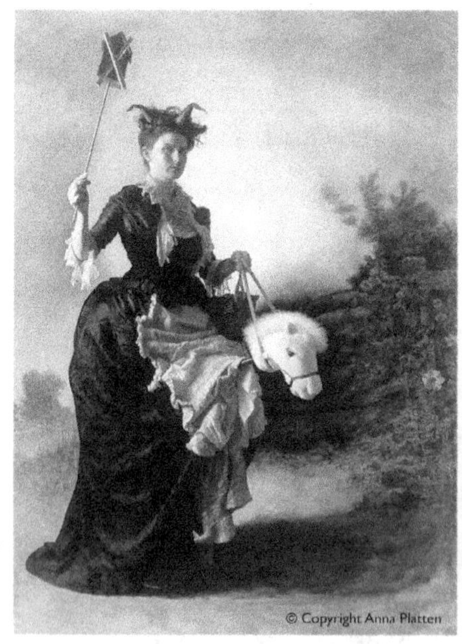

The Gate 2008

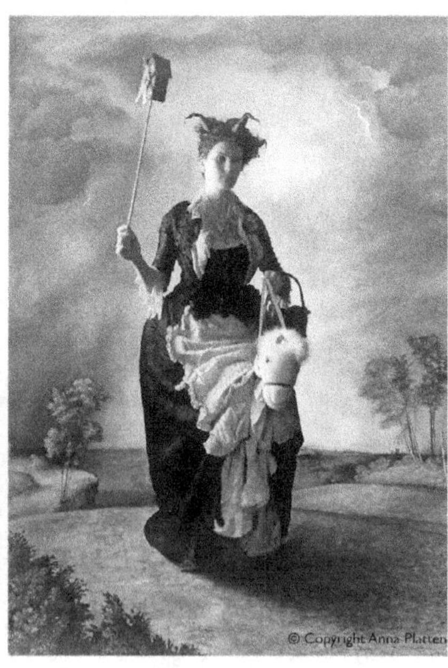

Thunder 2010

an engraving given to Anna by her sister; a sixteenth-century biblical illustration of the human soul as the wandering fool or jester. This engraving included the fool's hat, basket, hobbyhorse and windmill. Anna used the engravings content as inspiration to provide a visual link that helped to establish her character and to chart her travels across the landscape.

The woman's costume is an original Victorian dress Anna had found in a London op shop over 30 years ago, which gave authenticity to the paintings because of its obvious age. Not only the fact that it had been well worn, but it was appreciated by Anna because it enhanced the idea that the character had been travelling for a very long period of time. The figure stands in for anyone reflecting on the experience of passing through life, reflecting on one's long interaction with the *world within* and the *world without*. The colours she had used in the skies were so brilliant. She paints in a true renaissance style, with allegorical themes. I was in awe of her technique and the mastery with which she had managed to convey her own personal journey.

At the exit of the exhibition was a wall of photographs, which chronicled how she went about her craft and the making of props for her paintings. But the thing that struck me most was the fact we were born in the same year, and in that moment of recognition, I knew what I needed to do. I enrolled in art school and decided upon the art school which Anna's husband Rod Taylor founded in 1982, which is now a fully accredited university.

Little did I know at the time, was that an Arts degree would combine both psychology and art for me. The process of research-driven methodology to develop a body of work in the final year at art school led me to Carl Jung. Jung became my psychoanalyst - it was through my practical research of his work that opened the door to my introspective journey. Anna Platten became my mentor, and we eventually came to know each other through the art circles we both frequented. She is a highly private person, and so it is an honour to have her permission to include her extraordinary work in my book. Salvador Dali became my source for the methodology of Surrealism – owing to his being an interpreter of dreams! Frida Kahlo became my muse (she is also my favourite person to impersonate at parties!) Frida's one simple quote *'I paint self-portraits because I am so often alone, and I am the person I know best,'* sums up her authenticity and to which I could relate. I used myself as the reference of study, for this following body of work in my final year. And these people (Platten, Dali, Kahlo, Jung) were my teachers.

My return to art school was never about achieving a piece of paper (otherwise known as a Bachelor) at the end, rather it was the process of going back to school in my fifties that facilitated a return to who I was, through my love of art. In many ways, I was reconciling my life story. Where I had been, with where I was now, was going to determine my future.

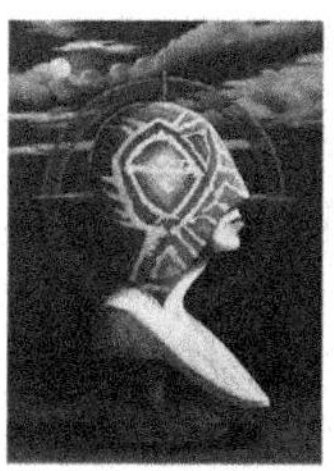 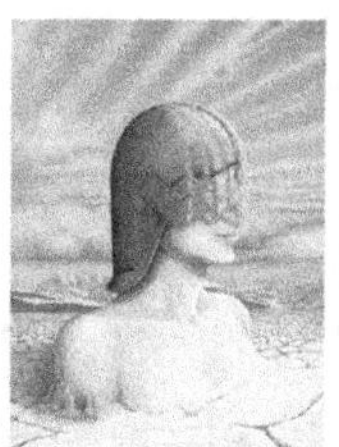 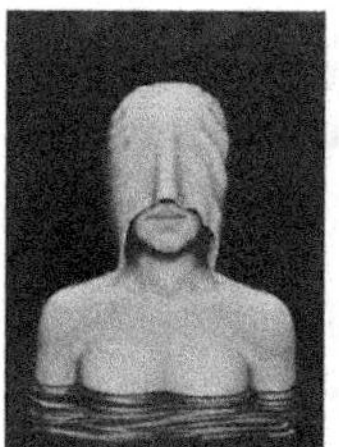 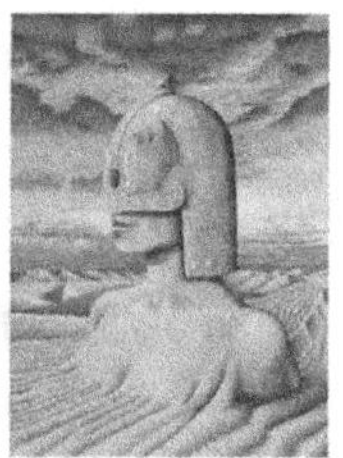 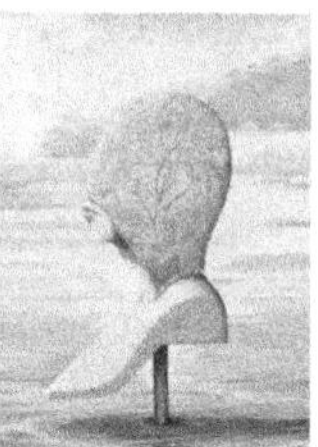

The Immortal Soul

Ten quotes by Carl Jung – I love this guy!

1. *The meeting of personalities is like the contact of two chemical substances; if there is any reaction, both are transformed.*
2. *The word 'happiness' would lose its meaning if it were not balanced by sadness.*
3. *If you are a gifted person, it doesn't mean that you gained something. It means you have something to give back.*
4. *The debt we owe to the play of imagination is incalculable.*
5. *There can be no transforming of darkness into light, and of apathy into movement without emotions.*
6. *What you resist persists.*
7. *We cannot change anything unless we accept it.*
8. *The privilege of a lifetime is to become who you truly are.*
9. *Knowledge rests not upon truth alone, but upon error also.*
10. *Until you make the unconscious conscious, it will direct your life and you will call it fate.*

Many of Jung's quotes deal with our own personal interpretation of the world around us. Jung believed the quality of our lives was related to the meaning we give to events, things, people and experiences. The quotes by Jung help us to reflect on how we function within the context of our surroundings. Meaning: Where do I fit in? What can I change? What will remain unchanged? What can I do to survive, and thrive in this environment? *Until you make the unconscious conscious, it will direct your life and you will call it fate*.

Through my investigations and research, I was drawn to the spiritual, the mythological, and the inner world of the human psyche. I always have been. Throughout the five years at art school, the recurring theme, which surfaced in all of my work, was that of the *unseen*. This was not a deliberate act; it's just what surfaced for me via the intuitive creative process, which led me to research and study Carl Jung.

Jung believed that the *Collective Unconscious* was an inherited collection of knowledge and images that every human being inherits at birth. People are unaware of the items contained in their *Collective Unconscious*. However, at times of personal crisis, the psyche may open a door to this realm. The images contained in the unconscious are frequently manifested in dreams. Jung believed that dreams provided an important window into the *Collective Unconscious* and that many symbols contained in dreams had a universal, uniform meaning to the whole of humanity.

According to Jung, the human *Collective Unconscious* is populated by instincts and by archetypes: universal symbols such as the Great Mother, the Wise Old Man, the Shadow, the Tower, Water, the Tree of Life, and such. Jung believed that the *Collective Unconscious* had a profound influence on the lives of individuals, who lived out the symbols, and which clothed them in meaning, through their experiences. That a *fantasy life* has a certain common basis for Jung's well-known theory of archetypes, where dreams have a structure similar to a fairy tale or a myth, which are the expression of a *Collective Unconsciousness.* Jung saw archetypes as the quintessential navigational tool of the psyche, providing a gateway between the conscious mind and the unconscious that could help us in becoming integrated human beings. He espoused that universal, mythic characters (archetypes) reside within the *Collective Unconscious* of people the world over. Today we now tend to refer to Jung's belief, quite simply as *The Collective*, as people become more accepting that we are all indeed connected as one united force.

I came to the conclusion through my research, that Archetypes are the psychic lens through which we view ourselves, and they are the vocabulary of intuition. Archetypes help us to express ourselves in our individual lives and influence how we connect to the real world. They help to balance our unconscious with the conscious and speak to us in a language of myths, symbols and signs.

Archetypes are the key to our personal power and cosmic intelligence, they are like putting on clothing you were destined to wear: Archetypal patterns are like a door into a hidden realm, a parallel reality of mythical proportions. My body of work titled *'The Immortal Soul'* is a sequence of five paintings, structured around the idea of personality archetypes as defined by Carl Jung. Depicted through the language of psychological, mythological, symbolic imagery and painted through the modality of Surrealism. They explore my life experiences and spiritual beliefs. Through the executioner's hood, I reflect on my existential view on life, and how I have reinvented myself many times over. The hoods, therefore, speak of endings and new beginnings. All the portraits of the archetypes explore the concept that humans have two basic natures, the physical and the spiritual. They represent psychic intuition: the unseen inner life, and guidance in the physical world.

I write about my self-portraits in the order by which I executed them. This was how they occurred to me, and ended up being a perfect chronological analysis of my life to date. In many respects, the imagery came very easily when I figured out what Archetypes I had been and which ones were still with me, but the analysis came later. Visually this is how I interpreted them. I was quite astonished at how healing the paintings were to me. I could articulate and view my life source through a mythical and symbolic lens. Even when I placed them up on my studio wall in their sequence, and viewed them, I felt this deep understanding (finally) of who I was. I am an artist, and this is my body of work - produced for my Bachelor of Visual Art.

The storytelling I have used to accompany the paintings are simply the stories I have linked to the chosen Archetype. Many cultures use storytelling to pass down cultural ideals through the generations. I, therefore, use the matriarch and patriarch from my own family, which of course informs my current existence. I tell the story of my illustrious career and share my private belief in reincarnation, - all the stories culminated in a cathartic process of delving deep within, through conversation with my Immortal Soul.

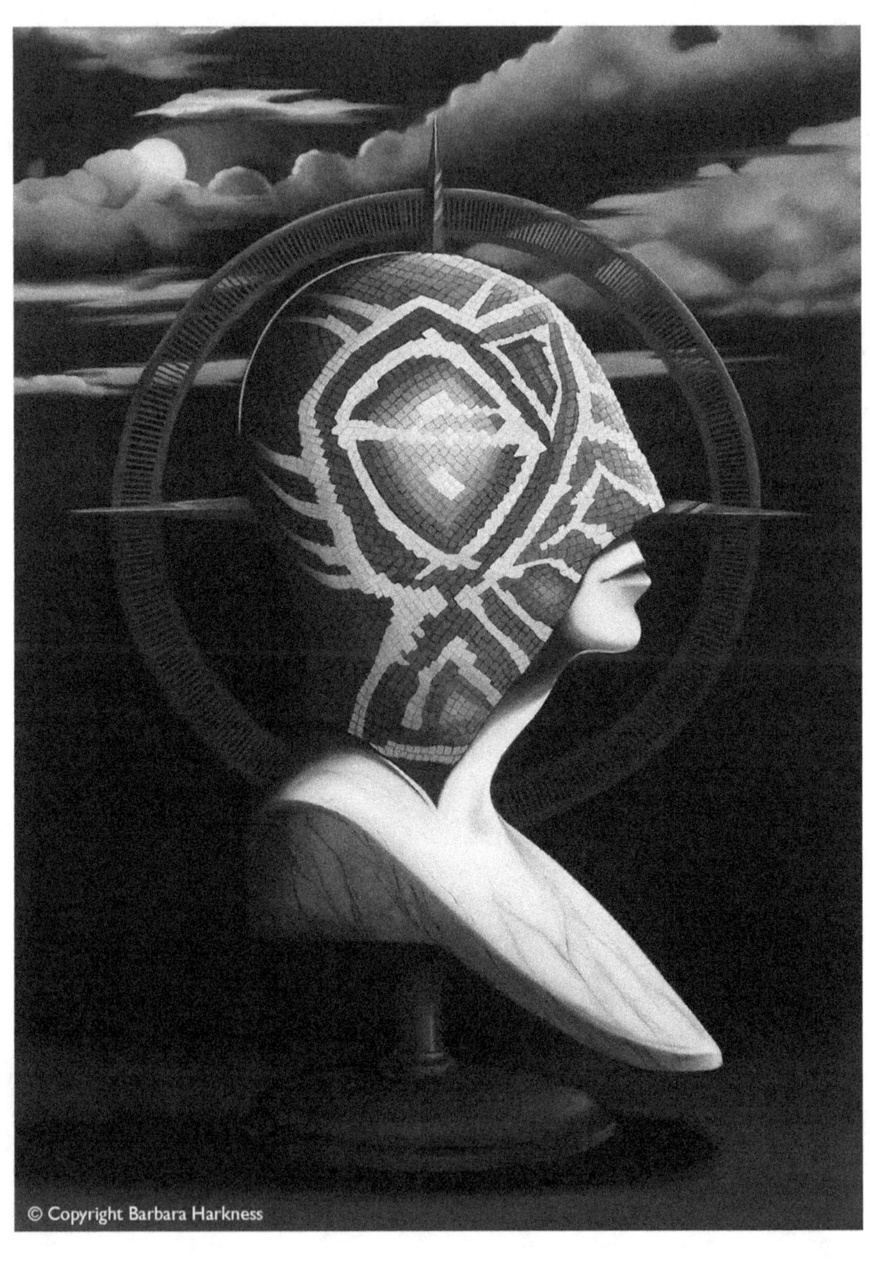

The Rebel

The Rebel & the Patriarch

"As far as we can discern,
the sole purpose of human existence
is to kindle a light in the darkness of mere being."
- Carl Jung

The Rebel Archetype; tells my story of *'The Dark Knight of the Soul.'* The painting reveals a strong masculine patriarchal link to history via the institutional marble bust, which speaks of old school and outdated male energy. The opposing and paradoxical nature of soft snakeskin over hard marble speaks of shedding the outmoded ideas of conformity. In cultural terms, snakes were regarded as immortal because they appeared to incarnate from themselves when they sloughed off their skins. They were also considered omens of fertility, wisdom, spiritual guidance and transformation.

The compass creates a visual halo of protection. Whilst the aspects of north, south, west and east are invisible, the subtle compass creates a visual armour of protection, directing the soul in the dark of night, guiding me in my darkest hour. The full moon heralds an ending. The moon's light shines brightly from behind the clouds, illuminating the subject – the soul, awaiting transformation.

The Rebel Archetype is a strong force to my persona, and I believe that this Archetype will reside with me for life. This particular painting references my childhood and adolescence. I was a rebellious child! I'm not sure if this was the result of being the third child, which bestowed upon me a feeling of being *undefined*, or perhaps it is just my souls' character? Of the four siblings, I had been the one lucky enough to have been born with a natural talent to draw and paint, yet this went unrecognised and unrewarded. I had an older sister, so she had that designated role, an older brother, who was the only and adored son, and a younger sister, who stole my thunder with her debut upon the earth, replacing my status as the youngest. I gave my parents rebellion in spades, in an effort to stand out and be recognised. Tantrums during my early years went unnoticed; they thought that by choosing to ignore me I would hopefully grow out of my dreadful affliction. Unfortunately, my father in particular could not deal with his rebellious daughter, and our relationship soured as I progressed into my teen years. This of course was my emerging adolescent Rebel, just getting stronger and more assertive. I ran away often in my younger years but always returned by nightfall. They never sent out the search party much to my dismay, even after I had shouted at them "I'll run away and you will never see me again"! By my teens I decided I would turn it up a notch and, to make them take notice of me, I stayed away for two whole days and nights (I was staying at a girlfriend's place) but they never cared to know who my friends were and therefore remained oblivious to my whereabouts. My sister and her boyfriend encountered me on the third evening, coming out from the movies, and held me prisoner until my father came to collect me. My father was convinced I had been with boys and to extract the truth from me, started to slap me when I would not answer him. This only made me more resolute in not giving him what he wanted. My truth was not what he believed anyway and I can still remember yelling at him - telling him how much I hated him, and to hit me again - asking for it!

This was my power over him; my hatred for my father was so deeply ingrained, I wonder to this day if there were karmic remnants from a past life that somehow crept into this one because, in many respects, I am not sure why I hated my father so much. This happened well before he ill-treated our mother, but perhaps I saw the subtle signs of emotional abuse and held him accountable as a growing and discerning adult. My mother eventually came to my rescue that night, because she thought he was going to kill me. My younger sister was cowering and crying in the corner, witnessing the whole ugly episode.

Oscar Wilde quotes: '*Children begin by loving their parents; after a time, they judge them; rarely, if ever, do they forgive them.*' Perhaps I wanted my father to love me more, but instead, I judged him. I know today that I could have changed our relationship by choosing to love him. But I couldn't do that, well not at that age. I didn't have the life tools to know how. But perhaps (a sliding door thought) if I had have given my father the love I had wanted so much, then my life would have also taken another path. He just might have loved me back and I would not have sought the kind of relationships I did from older men, as replacements for that void in my life.

At the time of revisiting this segment, I came to listen to a podcast by Jane Fonda, which was so relevant (let alone coincidental). Oprah Winfrey's series of Master Class talks by famous folk are based upon the knowledge that *life* is the best class we will ever allow ourselves to be taught in. Fonda states, *'that to know where we are going, we need to know where we've been. In that, we need to know who our parents were as well.'* Henry Fonda was emotionally disengaged towards his daughter, and yet she had such deep respect for the great man that he was. She stated that she adored him. Upon his deathbed, she confessed to wanting her father to tell her that he loved her, but instead, she said those words to him. He broke down and wept, and was still weeping when she left the room. She broke through. I have wondered now why my father reacted that way toward me and so I find myself quietly forgiving him in death because he was probably reacting in the only prescribed way he knew how. Men, don't beat your daughters - love them!

In his elderly years, my father became such a nasty old man and a chore to be around. He would not consider any home care and could not look after himself properly. His staple diet consisted of shoving a pork chop onto a dish and slow cooking it in the oven over four hours. My sisters were appalled at his living habits and general lack of hygiene, but not surprised when he got sick. He deteriorated pretty quickly; they put him into care, and waited for him to die. But he was a stubborn old man and the three months the doctors gave him turned into a year. There was much jibing in emails between us about *'hurrying up dad,'* because no one wanted to visit him any longer. My older sister dutifully took on this responsibility most weekends. My younger sister also couldn't tolerate him. I was thankfully living in another country, therefore absolved of my obligation. We had all felt quite angry over his treatment of our mother during their life together. In the end, she had shut herself away in her bedroom, from him and unfortunately the world as well. They never went out together, for he had replaced mum with a new girlfriend (he was about eighty at this stage).

Upon my mother's death, the girlfriend replaced that status as the doormat, and dad's treatment of her resulted in a call to my younger sister to ask if she could stop him from visiting her because he was getting nasty. If he didn't, then she was going to take out a restraining order against him! And so *the talk* to our father went something like this.

"Dad, Natalie doesn't want to see you anymore. She phoned and said that she doesn't want you to go around to her place anymore and hassling her."

"Rubbish, that's the first I've heard of it. Who says I can't visit her?"

"Natalie, she called me to pass on the message, because you won't listen to her."

"No, we're an item."

"No, you're not, she doesn't want to see you anymore."

"Bullshit, she likes me, and you can't stop me from visiting her."

"Well dad, suit yourself, but the police may get involved if you continue to make a nuisance of yourself."

Grunt!

It was not the first time that the police were involved with having to tell him off. One day he had become agitated while waiting behind a car, which was having difficulty pulling out into traffic, so he thought that he would shunt her along, just gently mind you! The lady was most upset (understandably) as she had a child in the car that was also very distraught at being shunted. Upon that visit from the police, and being told that he could no longer drive, he simply dug his heels in because he didn't like being told what he could and couldn't do. And so, my sisters disconnected the car battery, and he thankfully never worked it out.

I visited my father four months before he passed away. He did not show any signs of recognising me as his daughter. He had a black eye, which I don't believe was from walking into a door. He hated it in the home and made all of the interns know it. He was diagnosed with aggressive dementia, which explained a lot of his offensive behaviour.

He was most flattered that such a young thing (that's me) would pay him a visit. As I walked him arm in arm around the rest home grounds, he looked at me and said "You know, I'd turn for you, - if I saw you in the street, you'd make my head turn".

"Thanks, DAD". I emphasized the word DAD, whenever I spoke to him. The videos my sister took of him and me together were amusing to watch later on, as I could see a little smirk on his face at having some much-needed attention from a complete stranger.

The previous time I had visited my father, was a couple of year's prior. He had just turned the ripe old age of eighty and was still getting out and about. He had joined a singing group, whereby the folks involved would get up on stage and sing along with an accompanying band. I had persuaded my older sister into taking me to his special singing event to show some interest in his life. He had never shown any interest in ours, as children or as grown-ups. When we got to the club, he turned to us both and said "that will be $3 each, girls." My sister and I looked at each other and wondered why we'd bothered! But we waited patiently whilst all the other participants sang their lungs out, to the appreciative relies. It was sort of like a school concert in reverse, parents on stage, kids in the audience encouraging the extra-curricular, newly acquired hobby. Most were pretty average, but when my dad got up, I discovered a person I didn't know existed – he had the most beautiful voice!

He sang, *"I'm sending you a big bouquet of roses, one for every time you broke my heart."* His voice quivered as he sang, melodic, soft, and vulnerable. And I felt something instantly well up inside of me, this tidal wave of emotion, rise and rise until I could contain it no longer and I broke. Uncontrollable tears crashed upon the shore - sobbing, wracking tears. I had no idea where they came from, but somewhere in the deep recess of my soul, I felt my mother's pain, and that he was singing to her.

It was a song about romantic love, about going back, again and again, and it was also about saying sorry. The lyrics hit a chord with me. Was a part of my mother's spirit residing in me, resonating through me, connecting to me? All I know was this; what I felt, when I heard my father sing (considering my distant relationship with him) were not my feelings, but they overwhelmed me all the same. This is my attempt at trying to understand that moment, knowing what I know now, about the power of the soul at work, and the souls of our passed over loved ones.

Dad never accepted that he was at death's door, so when his body finally shut down, (probably through starvation, because he never ate) he finally admitted that he knew what was happening. It was confronting for my sisters to finally have this day arrive, even though we had all anticipated it for well over a year. My younger sister even forgave him for being so cruel to mum, held his hand and read him the Lord's Prayer as he took his last breaths. He died on the eve of my 57th birthday.

My parents' unhappy, painfully dysfunctional, yet enduring marriage was not an inspiring one. My father's dreadful, inconsiderate treatment of my mother was the one thing I was able to reconcile into a positive attribute for myself, and it made me strong enough to walk away with dignity from any relationship that did not feel right or showed signs of neglect and complacency. What I call the *'doormat effect'*.

I recognise the Rebel and know her well. I feel that the Rebel is innately, a much larger part of who I am, and though tamed somewhat now as a mature adult, the rebellious streak still surfaces now and then. However, upon reflection, I love this inner child with her strong sense of rebellion, so the Rebel will continue to stay with me throughout my life's journey, sloughing off skin after skin, to reinvigorate my soul's journey.

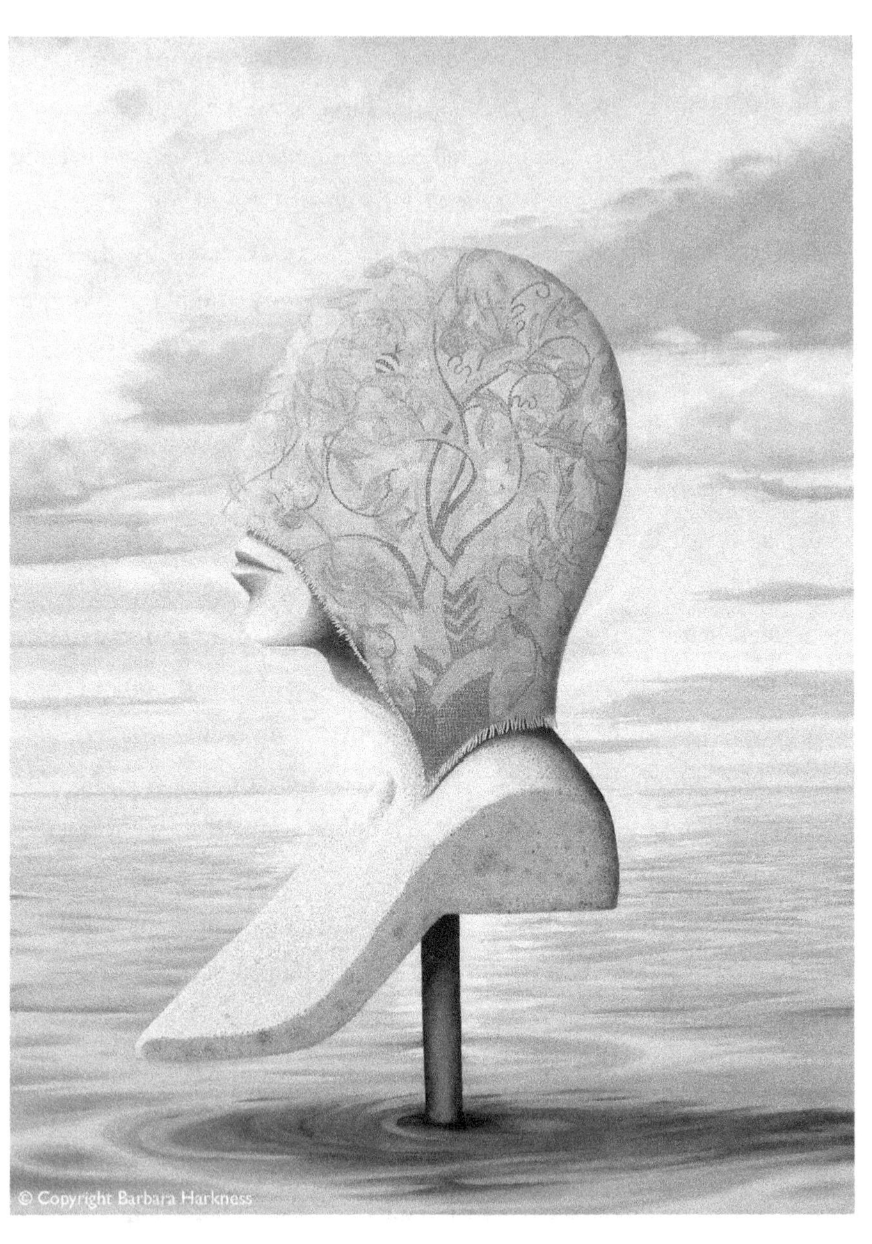

The Innocent

The Innocent & the Matriarch

"Where love rules, there is no will to power; and where power predominates, love is lacking. Each is the shadow of the other."
- Carl Jung

The Innocent Archetype; is the polarity to the Rebel. This painting represents the feminine with her soft sandstone bust growing from the life-giving sea. Innocent Eve opposing Satan in the Garden of Eden; she tells the story of creation, and as surely as night falls, so the sun rises to provide light and a brand-new day. The Innocent represents rebirth and a new beginning, from *'The Dark Night of the Soul'*. She is *'The Tree of Life'*. As a spiritual symbol, *'The Tree of Life'* crosses many cultures, representing ancestry, mythology, history, lineage and hope for the future. It carries the meaning that we are related to the cosmos, to our human family, our animal family, our earth family and our spiritual, ethereal family.

The words of Jane Fonda come to mind again; *'in that to know ourselves, we need to know our lineage*'. I have therefore chosen to weave my mother into the book. She has many stories of her own and deserves a place in my book as my father did, especially for all the good she represents in my life. My stories keep growing, as I write. Indeed, this process of discovery is endless. Now, the only maternal advice my mother gave me was this -*"get as far away from your family as possible, and start your own life"*, which I did. By understanding where she had been, I could therefore heed her words with the affection and goodwill she intended upon me with these words.

Let's go back in time to 1947: World War II had ended two years prior, a time which had engaged my mother as an entertainer in a dance troop, consisting of my mother Elsie, her sister Bessie and a friend called Lydia. Think *'Andrews Sisters and the Boogie Woogie Bugle Boy of Company B'* - their inspiration. Many a tale was told to me as a young child by my mum, of the war: London's bombings, the sirens, entertaining in the underground and emerging to the rubble from the bombs. On a positive note, however, she spoke more about the soldiers and the luxuries they brought the young ladies; chocolates, perfume, silk stockings. I remember my mother telling me how handsome and generous the men in uniform were, especially the Aussies and Americans.

Directly after the war, she became a bus conductress in London on the double-deckers. I am sure that she punched many a man's ticket (because she was so very cute), but a *ticket to ride,* was not meant for Elsie. When she discovered she was in the family way, she was promptly hidden from view. On September 17th 1947 my mother gave birth to a daughter and called her Margaret (more than likely in the hope that her mother would take her and the child in - my grandmother's name was Maggie). She had the child in an institution called Brocket Hall, a countryside estate that was turned over to the War Office during the war, then used as a maternity hospital directly afterwards. I guess there had to be some joy during wartime, and making love was obviously high on the list of activities. The London maternity hospital had also been destroyed during the war. Over 8,000 babies were born at Brocket Hall (exact figure 8338). These babies are now called the Brocket Babies and even have a website dedicated to them.

Elsie did keep her baby for three whole months, in the hope that her mother would accommodate both of them. Eventually, she gave the baby up for adoption. She succumbed to her mother's plan of starting a whole new life across the other side of the world. My mother boarded a boat for New Zealand, met her Prince Phillip shortly after arrival, and went on to have four children. It had worked for her; so, this was the best advice she could give to her Rebellious daughter. Interestingly, she never solicited this advice to my other siblings. I left New Zealand at seventeen, bound for adventure, creating and owning my life, and I never looked back.

The day my mother died, dad mentioned at the hospital that she had received news from a woman in England who believed she was related to her. The daughter my mother had given up for adoption 63 years ago had finally reached out to her. She had read the letter every day for a month, but such was the state of her dementia she probably thought it was a new letter every day. She never told anyone, but then she never told us about the baby she was forced to give up either. This was her secret and she managed to hide it from all four of us, swept under the carpet, as you did in those days.

The letter from her first daughter was polite and considerate of my mother's position in life. She did not want to upset anyone, she was mindful of the fact mum may not have mentioned to anyone the fact that she had adopted out her firstborn, to the point that she did not even state she was her daughter. But mum must have known who she was and continued to hide the letter, as she had her past and her pain. The letter came too late, as my mother had suffered a massive stroke and we (the children) had made the decision to not prolong her life owing to her dementia, and the state of her body's condition. And so, we let her slip peacefully into oblivion, with a good dose of morphine to aid the journey. We also knew that she was over it, and had wanted out for quite some time. The only escape from my father no doubt!

My poor dear mother suffered a nervous breakdown after Dad sent her packing at around their thirty-year marriage mark. This was the second time in her life that she had been discarded and sent on her way, first by her mother, then her husband. We had all left home by this time and she had no responsibilities apart from two grandchildren at the time. Her abolishment left her scarred, mentally and emotionally, and she was committed to a mental institution for six months. This was no mild nervous breakdown I hate to say, it was on the scale of a Mount Vesuvius eruption complete with being taken away in a straight jacket, put in a padded cell and administered shock treatment regularly. I don't believe she was the only woman of this generation who was committed for a nervous breakdown!

Mum had forgotten she had four children, and simply wanted her baby back. Didn't know who we were! All was revealed to us during those tumultuous months of incubation, and her secret was first revealed to us. I remember calling her from Australia and saying to her "mum, you don't belong in a mental institution".

To which she responded, "but everyone is so kind to me, I quite like it here."

I reiterate: that to know oneself, you have to know who your parents were. My mother's untenable and unbearable life with my father made me the strong and independent woman I am because I sure as hell didn't want to end up like my mother, who had no choices in life.

When I visited my mother in New Zealand in 2009, I knew that her time was close, and was not wrong for she passed away some four months later. Funny how I managed to visit both of them just before their passing, as it was also four months for my dad before he died also.

During that visit, I suggested to my sisters that we try and find her - our half-sister. surely with internet access these days making the world a village, the task would be easy. But mum didn't want a bar of it. Apart from her memory being quite vague, she was also of the opinion that too much water had gone under the bridge, and the prospect did not excite her, and so we let it be.

Little did we know, however, that what was happening in the northern hemisphere at exactly that time was the initiation of a search by our half-sister. Months of research, trawling relatives in Scotland that bore her name revealed nothing, until a second search of the boats which had left the UK regularly after World War II with immigrants to populate Australia and New Zealand, revealed my mother's name. My half-sister had not necessarily needed to find her birth mother, being perfectly happy with her adoptive parents and respectful of their position in this regard. However, my mother's name was on her birth certificate, and I guess curiosity got the better of her. In this case curiosity was all it probably amounted to, as my half-sister did not need to know the details of *'why.'* Considering the era, it was pretty normal for young mothers who were unmarried to give their babies up for adoption. Once her location was discovered a private detective in New Zealand was employed to trace her whereabouts and upon confirmation, provided her address to her adopted daughter, albeit too late.

On one of my trips to London I met up with my half-sister and we delved through the adoption documentation of discovery she had in her possession. One of the most poignant facts revealed was that mum's sister Bessie (also from the dance troop) gave birth to a son, just one day after Elsie, in their mother's home. The difference between Bessie and Elsie of course was her status. Bessie was married! How unbelievably hard that must have been for my mother, knowing that their kids, as cousins, could have had a relationship, and their dance days would have been cemented even further through the children they had borne within hours of each other. My heart ached for my mother when I knew she had given up a child after three months of cuddling and knowing her. I finally understood her pain of being exiled, when she had so much to gain from the circumstances of the family connections surrounding her at that time.

Nine months after the birth of her daughter my mother caught a boat to New Zealand, to start a new life. She was 27 years old. She went on to have three more daughters, one son, six granddaughters and three grandsons, and was remembered fondly by all as this gorgeous little Scots woman, with a flair for singing and dancing, and making a hoot n' nanny raucous with her clan.

The raw hessian nature of The Innocent with its intricate tapestry hood depicting '*The Tree of Life*', heralds a time when I was innocent and crafting a new life as a young woman. I met my first husband shortly after arriving in Australia; we fell madly in love and began creating a life together. These were my beautiful, productive and innocent years; having children, nurturing them, and creating a wonderful home environment for all of us. This was my conditioning, and I was very excited about having my own family. I loved being married, I loved being pregnant, I loved being a wife, I loved my two little boys when they arrived in my life, and I was grateful for all of it. My life was better than I could have ever hoped for. Mother was right!

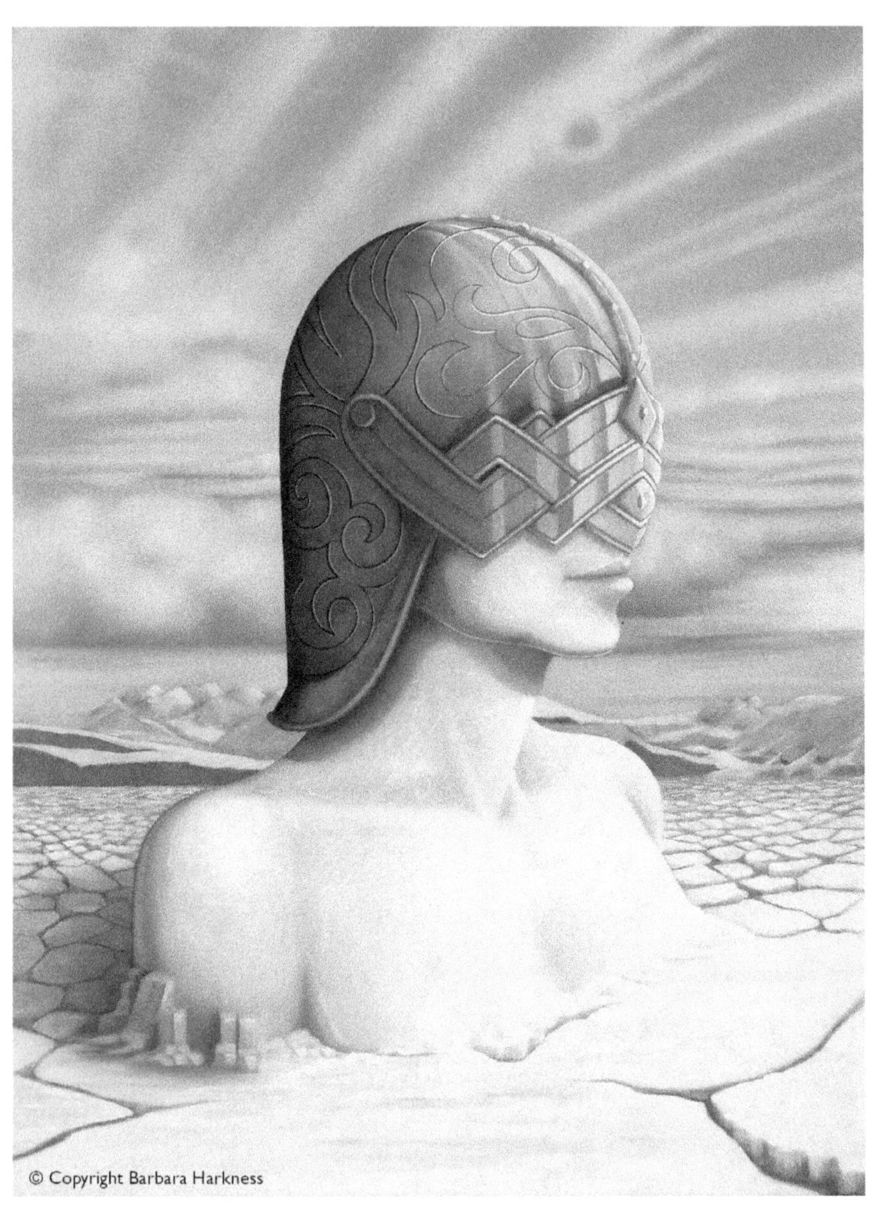

The Ruler

The Ruler – in Business

"I am not what happened to me,
I am what I choose to become."
- Carl Jung

The Ruler Archetype; through the story of this powerful Ruler/ Queen Archetype, I explore a period of 20 years when I was a business owner and a leader. This was a highly defining time in my life, which gave me huge amounts of self-confidence. I am the Ice Queen, appearing in an ephemeral environment of cracking ice. She has been sculpted from ice, just as I carved out a career for myself, which evolved into a thriving business and prosperous life. The nature of cracking or melting ice does, however, suggest the possibility that it could all too easily slip away, and so caution also needs to be exercised - because this is the fickle real world of *business*.

I could not relate anything mythical to running a business, because I was operating very much in the real world. Game of Thrones was my escape at the end of a hard day's work, so perhaps this was my connection to the mythical world, which has certainly influenced the imagery! Yes, they were indeed the battle years of my life, where I validated my worth by financially providing for myself. I remember feeling that I had to do this, because I had never been financially independent, and so this strong independent force fuelled my desire to succeed. Ego had a lot to do with it too, and in this regard, I feel *ego* has had a pretty bad rap of late. *'ego, it's just a dirty word,'* - is it? Perhaps the ego is how we decipher ourselves in the world, in society, like a judgment system, especially when it comes to our careers, and how we gauge ourselves to others. Perhaps that's what having a healthy ego is really about?

During my design career, I was also a teacher to young designers whom I mentored until they were ready for the larger world of design agencies. These young designers I employed straight from design school and built my company upon this philosophy. Yes, they were cheaper to employ, but I also enjoyed their youthful enthusiasm and willingness to learn from me. I built a team of wonderful young designers; none of whom stayed more than four years, and I didn't expect them to. I felt very privileged when one of those junior designers knocked on my door one day (years after he had left) to thank me for teaching him so much, which in turn enabled him to secure a really good job in London. The fact that he came to thank me was my reward. I was able to show my sons how to build a small business (and create a life) by example. "Between the years of thirty to sixty, build your empire, make your mark in the world, and stop playing around, because these are the years that set you up. You can relax later, in the comfort of your mature years, and be proud of the life you gave yourself," I told them.

I launched the company JUST ADD WINE by mid-1999, ten years after I'd started consulting to wine vignerons as an independent freelance wine label designer. I had morphed into somewhat of a *branding expert*, with no deliberate knowledge of this ideal. However, I accepted the flow of where my ideas took me and was provided for handsomely as a result.

In early 1999, a wine marketing conference held in Adelaide focused on developing export markets for Australian wine. It certainly captured my attention. The conference was initiated by wine marketing gurus from New Zealand, who was just beginning to forge their way in the international market with a clean, green marketing strategy for its premium cold climate wines. They used that environmental hook to sell their burgeoning wine industry to the rest of the world. The kiwi wine gurus suggested deploying the concept of *Brand Australia* - our sunshine, the unique animals, and the tourism imagery that Australia is renowned for. The clean and green marketing was working for the New Zealand wine industry, but we needed a strategy to sell into an export market. Tourism was already strong in that regard, so why not expand upon that unique proposition?

The tax-effective planting schemes of the mid to late 1990s meant that Australia now had a massive problem with an over-supply of grapes, and needed to find new markets desperately for all the pending wine which was flooding the market in oversupplied proportions – and we all know what that means! I remember walking away from that conference with the germination of an idea. Most of my clients were small-time vignerons, for whom I had created a label for their family enterprises. They were all now at the same stage with their business developments and needed to export their product with the surplus of wine currently in the market. Not wanting to compromise their existing brands' value, it made sense to create a completely separate one primarily for export. The idea of selling *'Brand Australia'* was a powerful message, and it stuck with me. And that is how JUST ADD WINE (the new company I created for this venture) was born.

My one employee (at the time) and I created a portfolio of Aussie style labels, complete with names and brand stories, and presented them as digital images loaded up onto a website, accessible to select clients, via a password, who could then view the concepts to purchase off the shelf. Like choosing a bottle of wine, my clients could simply choose a design, rent it for a fee, rather than pay a full design commission, for their export purposes. They were basically renting the concept on a thirty or sixty-day plan to market their wine into a selected country of choice or to find a distributor to take them on. Having a specific label design was a *value-added* proposition, which completed the business offering, rather than sending just wine samples. The designs were unabashedly Australian, they were fun, they were quirky, they were cheap, and they displayed sunshine on a bottle at a price point, which was also appropriate to the quality of the surplus wine available.

This was also a completely new way of working for Graphic Design companies. I got a lot of flak from other designers who thought I was compromising the industry and thought it was akin to free pitching. But this was quite different in fact, and I employed four junior designers who were eager for the experience of being able to use their core creativity rather than designing to brief driven projects. I was the original forerunner to this innovative way of working, and for my success in the game was nominated as a Central Regional finalist in Ernst & Young's Entrepreneur of the Year, 2005.

The [yellow tail] concept was the first horse out of the gate, sold in the Qantas lounge just an hour after JUST ADD WINE was launched into Sydney, and to the first person it was pitched to. Now for legal reasons I shall not mention the company name, however as the owner of the moral rights to the brand (being its creator) I am entitled to tell my side to the story. He was the marketing manager for a medium-sized wine company and was actually on his way to the USA for a crucial meeting about pulling their current brand from the market, owing to lack-lustre sales. He probably knew that providence had just stepped in, because he could now go to that meeting with confidence, knowing that he had a pretty good backup plan. It was not *sold in* however until we put together a full marketing strategy for the sales pitch to the USA importer. I worked on the packaging component, which included a full rollout of the label, from the brand story and tag line to all point-of-sale material. They pulled out all the guns with promotional sell in incentivising merchandise, which included Driza Bone coats and Akubra hats, all emblazoned with the quirky [yellow tail] imagery.

At the sell-in of [yellow tail] to the USA importer, the marketing manager donned the Aussie gear and carried a two-bottle carry case with Australia's two icon wine varieties, (Chardonnay and Shiraz) dressed in the [yellow tail] label. Now the importer was a family business, which is why they liked dealing with another *family-sized* business. A level-playing field, so to speak. And so, it was easy for the importer to say quite frankly what he thought of the new proposition. They were not impressed with the frivolity of a concept named [yellow tail], along with the fact it had a kangaroo on the label!

"You don't honestly expect me to sell this, do you?" they responded. But the importer had a son (thankfully) who understood the concept of selling *'Brand Australia.'*

"I like it," he said, "I think it has legs!"

It sure did, as it bounded into the market with a punch, and the rest, as they say, is history. Rock star [yellow tail] with a rebel yell, shouting *'look at me, look at me'* entered the market, hit the charts in record speed time, and soared to dizzying sales heights. Within two years of the launch [yellow tail] had become America's number one selling brand, and showed no signs of slowing down. Recent research shows me that in 2021 it is still the world's most powerful wine brand. There you go - the brand that literally saved the Australian wine industry over-supply problem, by soaking up the majority of Australia's excess grape production, was my baby!

Now a reasonable figure for any first-year shipment of wine into a new market is around 25,000 cases – that's considered pretty good. [yellow tail] in its first year did over 100,000 cases, and in its second year of production, sales reached 1.2 million cases - which was how it gained its reputation as a phenomenon. However, a consolidation between Southcorp and Rosemount's distribution networks also provided a gap in the market for a new player to enter, and the perfect storm for [yellow tail] to sail into. The brand made worldwide history as the fastest growing wine brand ever launched and appeared in university textbooks as a Blue Ocean case study. [2]

The marketing manager who purchased the concept at that fateful airport meeting also knew the power of a good story. He sold in the fact it was a concept purchased off the shelf, and not concocted by ad men, nor put out to market research for approval or confirmation of its sex appeal. The accompanying story of course was me, and the fact that it was purchased in such a way, off the shelf, without a brief, the whole kit and caboodle. This was innovation; a new way of working for graphic designers, which in turn created a trail of copycat companies (the highest form of flattery of course). But I was the first and original company to instigate working this way, and it gave power to the graphic design industry as a profession, for we were doing what we did best – designing without the constraints of briefs so tight and conformed that the labels basically designed themselves.

Regardless of the fact I *forgot* to ask for royalties was not why I

---

[2] Uncontested market space, where differentiation and low cost make the competition irrelevant.

created JUST ADD WINE. The success of [yellow tail] provided growth in my small business, employing young designers who were eager to learn under my tutorship. I enjoyed my team and our innovative approach to design solutions for the wine industry. We became trailblazers and were highly sought after for our innovative concepts. I worked intuitively, and I believe that my idea of selling *'Brand Australia'* was an integral part of the success behind [yellow tail]. There is nothing so powerful as an idea whose time has come - right! It was Innovative, Innocent and Intuitive. The three 'i's of design which contributed to [yellow tail] blindsiding the wine industry the way it did. It was not the five P's that were cited as responsible for [yellow tail]'s success: Product, Promotion, Price, People, and Packaging (yep packaging comes in last!) It was also never intended to be a Rock Wallaby, just because we have a yellow-footed wallaby in our vast repertoire of Australian animals does not mean that [yellow tail] was a far-flung distant cousin! It's a WINE LABEL, and wine is this crazy drink, which makes you tiddly and relaxed (in moderation). It was just a memorable, quirky name, which had no literal meaning at all, and never needed to be justified. It was Australian, and it screamed the fact, that's all! Now I personally believe that one of the reasons [yellow tail] connected to the American consumer, was through its indigenous subtleness. It had an indigenous look and feel to it, which sold in *Australia.* And the name had a subtle North American indigenous connotation, you know, like; me - [yellow tail], you -{running bear}! The design connected with the consumer, which is what a designer's job is.

Journalists, from Australia to New York, contacted me for interviews about my point of view on [yellow tail], and in particular, the question about why I was NOT receiving royalties became a hot topic. Well of course I was just a tad miffed about *forgetting* to ask. Who in their right mind wouldn't be just a bit upset about leaving out a crucial clause, especially if the brand was going to be such a huge ongoing success? I could have just sat back and reaped in a tidy income every year for life - doing absolutely nothing! This seemed to be such a sell in point for the interviews and I got asked the question over and over again. But not even I knew, nor ever anticipated the wild success the brand would enjoy. The stories they wrote always favoured the point of view that the label was the *success* of the product, and without it (as had been the case with its bland predecessor) it would not have reached the heights it did. When one journalist asked me what I thought of the wine, I had to honestly reply that I had never tried it because [yellow tail] was not sold in Australia at this time. It was designed as an export label and sold as such until they decided to market it on home base as well.

"You mean they have never even sent you a case? I would have thought they'd have you on tap with a yearly supply, just as a thank you gesture at the very least!" And they published the point.

This really annoyed the owners of [yellow tail], and as a result, obliterated me from any further communication in the [yellow tail] story. They were also seemingly aggravated that the label, the name, and the story behind it being an off the shelf purchase, seemed to get more mention than the wine. Now I will be the first to admit that the label will sell the bottle in the first instance, but the product inside will keep the consumer coming back for more, time and time again. Its driving success was the wine, but, unfortunately, they were sore about the fact the packaging gained more attention. A sorry fact I personally think they should have acknowledged with gratitude, and not the newly instated story about how *they* created the name and commissioned me to design the label for them, along with the fact they promoted it with a $24 million marketing campaign. Yeah, well not in the first instance they didn't. No one would put that sort of money behind a new product, because it's always a great big dart-throwing exercise at the beginning with any wine brand. Some stick and some don't. The campaign came later, once they knew they had bought the winning lottery ticket and had the booty to reinvest in the brand.

As the original creator of the concept, I would always retain the moral rights to [yellow tail], however, their displeasure with my attachment to the brand did not stop there. When I tried to launch my growing business into Sydney by opening an office in this state, I used the tagline *'Come and meet the creators of the world's fastest-growing brand, [yellow tail]'* in the marketing campaign. As a result, I received a call from the marketing manager, who politely warned me that they would appreciate my not associating my company name with the [yellow tail] brand. I was told that I could refer to the usage of the word *'label'*, but clearly stated that they were the creators of the *'brand.'* Fair point, but sore point too!

I loved being associated with [yellow tail], because it was my inception, my creation, and it did define me for a good section of my life. I became a keynote speaker at many conferences, delivering on the power of good branding and [yellow tail] was always the requested topic. I would talk about the marketing of *'Brand Australia'* and how this was implemented into all their marketing and merchandising, much of which I was NOT responsible for, such as the [yellow tail] train. Every week (actually it might even have been a couple of times a week) a huge double semitrailer would leave the winery with bright yellow canvas sides emblazoned with the [yellow tail] branding, to take the wine to the port of Sydney. Apparently, it was quite a sight to behold. They never missed an opportunity that's for sure, and I was proud of how powerful and impactful the brand was. I was so pleased that it provided jobs to so many industries associated with wine. I was happy that it turned a little, unknown winery at the time, into the second-largest producer of wine in Australia today; they were absolutely the right buyers for that brand because they had a specific mission as well, - to be just that. My peers respected me for my contribution to the wine industry, for the fact that such a powerful brand was precisely what was needed at the time to soak up the wine surplus.

The years from 1990 to 2005 were the halcyon days of the wine industry, and I was a large part of that era. Everyone made a lot of money, and the parties and long lunches were frequent and great fun; these were the spin-offs in the wine industry, food + parties + wine = good times! The wine industry also had a wonderful *grapevine* system, which was how my business launched in the first place (no social media back then) and most inter-business promotion was done through good old-fashioned word-of-mouth. If you did a good job they sang your praises, and you got referred for the next job, and the next. This also worked adversely of course. However, I never chose to be a wine label designer, but when that opportunity presented itself to me, I knew instinctively that I had to go through the door. My career as a designer was more about making my own way in life and surviving in the world by my own volition. Wine label design chose me and I call that fate, it was not my destiny. It defined me for a good twenty years, and I shall always be grateful for the life I built through the success of the business. However I did not want my epitaph to read; *'Here lies [yellow tail] designer, gone but not forgotten, even though she 'forgot' to ask for royalties!'*

It was quite simply, time for a re-birth!

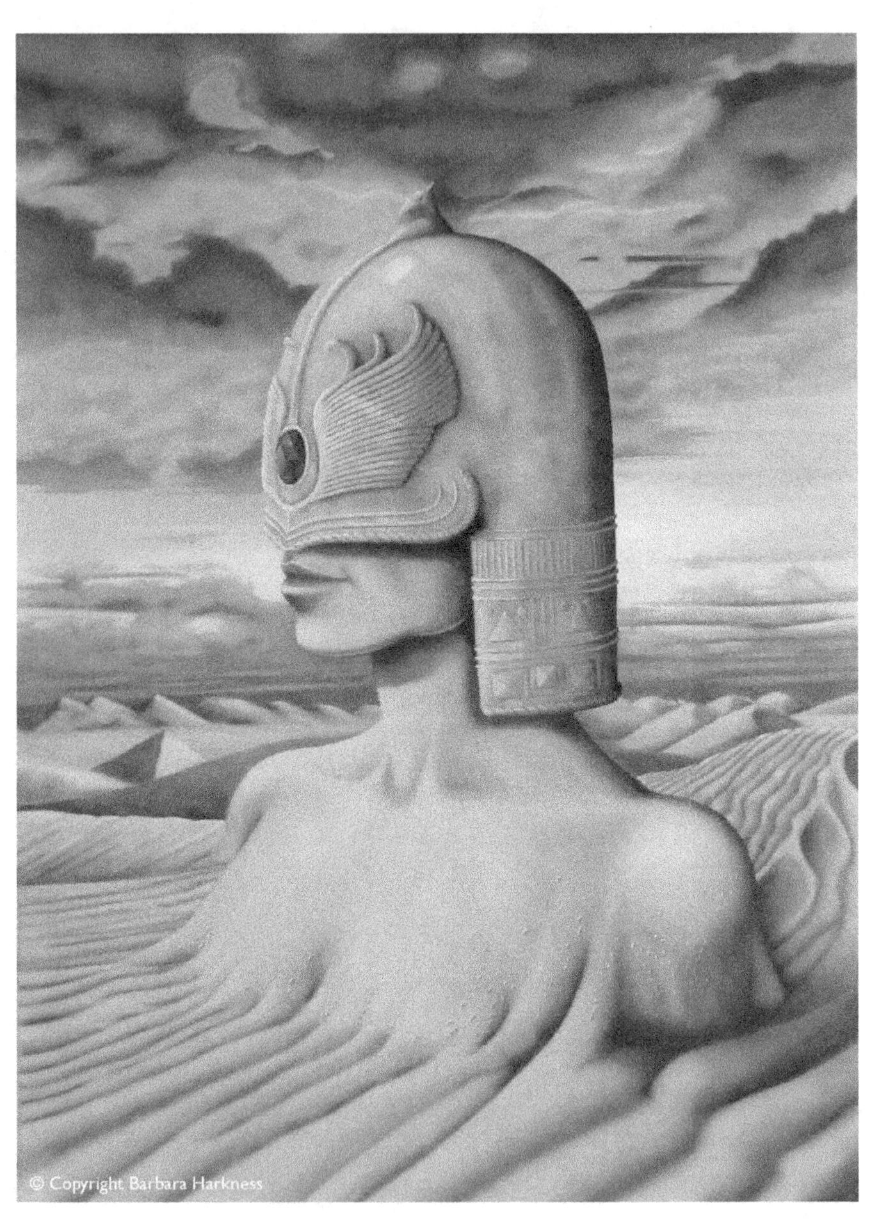

The Creator

The Creator – Phoenix rising, a new life

"A man who has not passed through the inferno of his passions has never overcome them."

- Carl Jung

The Creator Archetype; I believe that the archetypes we relate to are clothing for the soul and that we transition sometimes from one Archetype to another as we travel through our life journeys. Painting the Archetypes which I have been, and through the process of self-analysis, was such a cathartic exercise of discovering who I am and who I had been. A reconciliation of sorts! Studying Jung's Archetypes also made me realise that our growth as humans is sometimes about trying on these Archetypal clothes, with the freedom to move on to the next suit of armour. Which is precisely what I did when I handed my business on to my son. The changing of the guard, and the regenerative generation was ready to take control. I relinquished my Ruler Archetype to the new order and donned my new attire with the aplomb of a Phoenix rising, ready for a new life.

The Creator archetype trusts in the creative process above all else and lives for authentic self-expression. Typically, they are inventors, entrepreneurs, writers and artists, who like to contribute to society by realizing a vision by bringing something into being. They derive deep satisfaction from both the process and the outcome of creating something that did not previously exist. Inherently non-conformist and sometimes self-involved, this archetype desires freedom of expression and doesn't like to feel stifled.

Both the Ruler and Creator represent my creative careers, past and present. The present Creator Archetype is currently under construction, hence the depiction of a giant sand-castle-sphinx-like figure in the landscape. As a teller of stories, I have chosen to spin a tale based on one of my personal beliefs – reincarnation. Whatever the quality of the Creator is; writing, painting, designing, this is my new career and I have known of this dexterity from a very early age. I have spun a good tale about my design career, because [yellow tail] is a damned good story and largely defined that segment of my life as a designer. The Creator is about my burgeoning career as an artist; which is still a work in progress! In total juxtaposition to the Ruler, I sought to depict warmth; because I needed my life to glow again. I was in build mode, and in the process of literally reinventing myself!

My research led me to the mythical tale of the *'The Rising of the Phoenix'*. The Egyptian, Greek, Chinese, Japanese, Indian, Aztec, Persian, Assyrian and even the Jewish civilizations all had their unique cultural versions but was always known as *'the Bird of the Sun and Fire'*, which had a special ability to rebirth after a long period of time. This may very well be the *Collective Unconscious* that Carl Jung refers to as *'a binary invisible force between cultures of the world'*. Jung believed that all civilisations were interconnected.

I will, however, reference the Greek version for clarity of the story; *'The Mythical Phoenix Bird'* was known to have regenerative powers that were both invincible and immortal. Associated with the sun, the Phoenix obtains new life by arising from the ashes of its predecessor. When the Phoenix bird tires of life, it creates a nest of frankincense and Myrrh, self-combusts into flames, and is burned to ashes. Shortly after, the *Phoenix* rises again and begins its life anew. There are different traditions concerning the lifespan of the Phoenix, but by most accounts, the Phoenix lived for 500 years before tiring of its existence and feeling the need to re-birth.

The Phoenix today represents power and resilience, a universal symbol of rebirth and the beginning of a new cycle. People have used the *Phoenix* in many poetic and creative ways to express themselves owing to this fact, which is how I came to choose this myth to project myself as *The Creator Archetype.*

The introspective process led me to delve into ideas of reincarnation. I have no proof of this concept of course, and perhaps it is easier to accept that we don't exist after death and our body eventually returns to dust. However, I find that concept just as hard to accept, quite simply because I cannot imagine my consciousness not being present in the now, which of course is also the past and the future. In many respects I was accessing my imagination in ways I never had before. *Imagination* definition: *the act or power of forming a mental image of something not present to the senses or never before wholly perceived in reality.* There was definitely something more than my *minds' imagination* going on here! Which led me to ask *'was my soul making the art, which provided the answers I was seeking'?*

The Creator is set into a hot landscape with the searing sun burning brightly in my life, the polarity to the Ice Queen Ruler. With my birthstone (a sapphire) installed into the gold helmet as a third eye, this indicates the opening awareness of a sixth sense. Am I accessing the primal innate creative qualities of possible past lives? The Creator story is my personal interpretation about reincarnation, told as a past life.

My spiritual guide, Amreeta Stara, was a woman I had met a few years prior who performed all types of spiritual guidance, including past life regressions. She loved doing these regressions and I think that somehow, she saw the projections I couldn't. It was explained to me that I would feel lucid throughout the experiment and that I would not necessarily see images, but would *feel* the experience instead.

I sat in a recliner chair with a mask over my eyes. She led me into a trance, with soft music whilst counting down in reverse to zero. Through a method utilised by the Akashics, she transitioned me from current reality to the library of my past lives. I entered into a realm, which felt either Mayan or Egyptian. There was a temple with stairs, which I ascended. The temple was boxy at the top and not pointed like a pyramid. I was asked what era I thought I was in and replied, "600." I didn't know whether it was BC or AD, it was just a figure, which came to me, and quickly I might add. I was dressed in a white robe with a gold belt and carried a small child who was my son. At the top of the stairs was a platform, which overlooked the land beyond, and upon the land were hundreds of people. They were my people, and I seemed to have some sort of higher status because as I appeared, they all dropped to their knees. There was an eerie silence from the crowd - as they observed me holding my child, transfixed and in some sort of reverent ritual of prayer. In fact - they seemed upset! This naturally gave me the impression that this was a sad day. I then went inside the temple, which was full of important priests and other dignitaries waiting for me. Everyone was dressed in white robes, and again there was an eerie silence, with all eyes upon me. The child was taken from me and I walked to the altar.

At this stage, I faltered in my telling of events. I don't know where it all came from and I kind of felt like I was making it all up from movies I'd seen, like Raiders of the Lost Ark! Seeing that I had stopped, my guide asked me to look down and describe the shoes upon my feet. I instantly described the shoes, which had curled up toes. Thinking I must have got the countries screwed up and was actually in China, totally threw me off course. She then asked me to go to my death at the end of that life - and at this point my concentration became laboured and forced. For I saw myself in a bed with my family all around me, dying from good old age. I also knew that it was wrong, which broke the connection of course. My guide indicated that maybe it will come to me at a later time, and she encouraged me to call her if I *remembered* my end.

When I got home that afternoon I Googled a few things for clarity. Firstly, Egypt 600BC, and then Egyptian shoes. Guess what! The commoners wore rattan sandals, and the higher classes wore shoes with curled up toes, and these different types of footwear determined a person's status. This was the only indication that my story had any credibility! The following day I woke with the details of my death in that life. It was not a dream, but a knowing, and it all made sense - to me!

That day in the temple was the day of my death and I was walking to the altar to be sacrificed. I was a person of some high status. My child had been born out of wedlock, but I had not divulged the knowledge of the father, who was a mere commoner, and he would have been killed for his deed of fathering my child. He had also absconded upon hearing of my pregnancy. To purify the future of my son, a sacrifice needed to be made. Being as the father could not meet that obligation (coward) it was deemed better for the child that he did not know of his bastard heritage and therefore all evidence needed to be eradicated through my sacrifice.

I know, I know, pretty far-fetched isn't it! Research about Mayan

Sacrifices was the closest I could find to validate my story. For there was a stone bed at the altar in my vision, and it was upon these stone beds that the person was laid, tied by their arms and feet to all corners of the table and their heart extracted whilst still beating. No wonder I could not go there! Apparently, the Mayans loved a good bloodletting ceremony and the higher the status of the sacrifice… the happier the gods were.

The Egyptians on the other hand didn't seem to perform these rituals but did sacrifice slaves for continued duties on the other side when a pharaoh died.

I thought that the shoes were a pretty cool sign!

I have never done this again. I simply thought it was an interesting experience, which only served to offer up more questions than answers about reincarnation….

Was this my soul's storytelling, because I asked the questions? I believe my soul revealed this story to me for the purpose of bringing my persona and my soul into closer alignment. As these aspects of self, seek to find their place within the characteristics that make up the human condition, it served to add to my self-belief that I was on track in this lifetime, and in a new incarnation as *A Creator*.

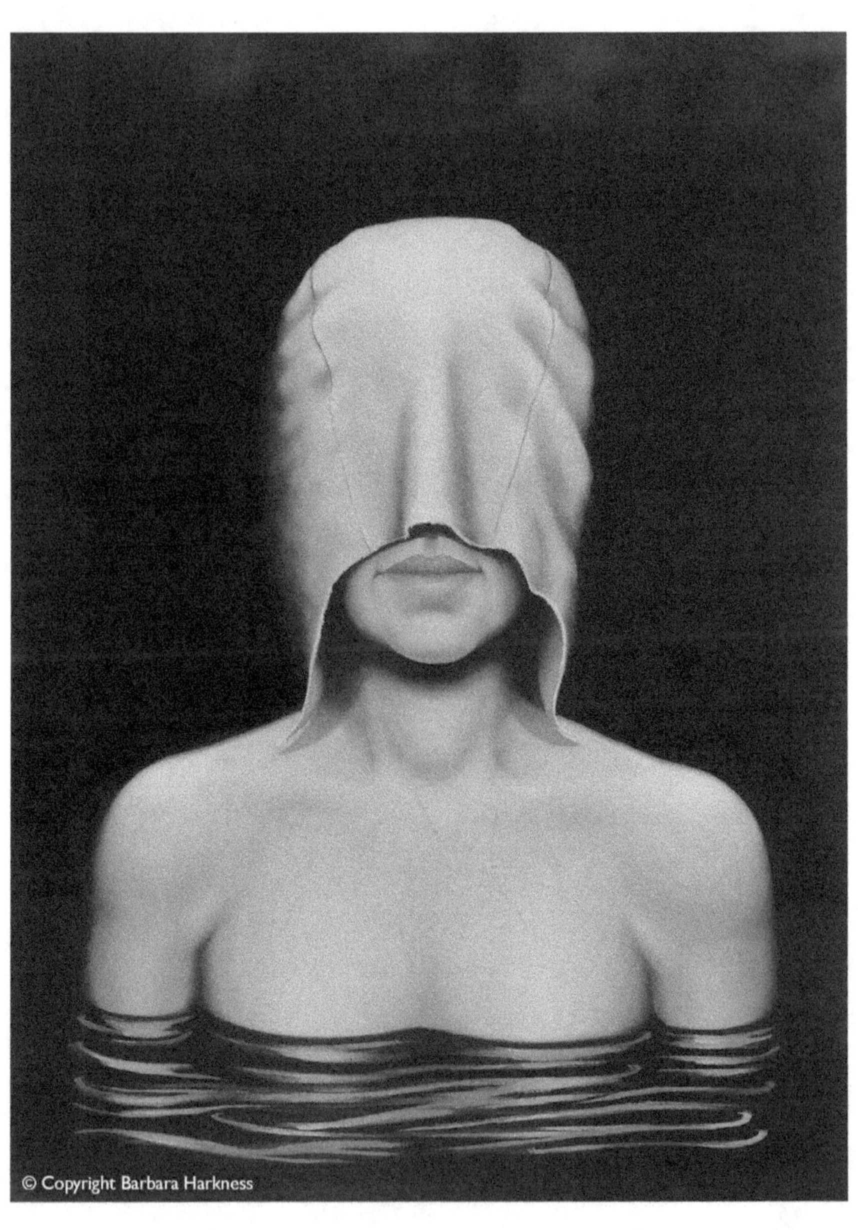

The Visionary

The Visionary - Manifesting Magic

"Your visions will become clear only
when you can look into your own heart.
Who looks outside, dreams; who looks inside, awakes."
- Carl Jung

The Visionary Archetype; This Archetype has a special ability to sense two forces that are constantly operating in their lives, both individually and collectively. They bring the future into the present through their ideas. The Rebel and Visionary Archetype often go hand in hand, as they are often considered the engines of change. The Visionary archetype feels limited by traditional systems, constrained by conventional rules and regulation, and smothered by familiar ways of doing things. They usually seek to create their occupation, not step into an existing one.

Elon Musk comes to mind as a person who has both these Archetypal traits. Steve Jobs is another. On a larger scale, these people forge a better world through their inspiring ideas and motivation for a better world. On a far humbler scale, such as my own, the commitment to an idea that has the power to transform me is a vision worth nurturing.

Myths speak to the Visionary more directly than most other Archetypes. Symbols and images are the language of the soul to the Visionaries inner world.

Caroline Myss describes in her book dedicated completely to

articulating the Archetypes[3], *"that the vision quest – with its promise of transformation, rightly belongs in the category of spiritual myths. The vision quest is a rite of passage, an inner journey to awaken a seeker's visionary sense. In these traditions, the quest for inner truth and integrity is valued above all else. The vision quest awakened within the Visionary, provides such a clear awareness of who she really is, that betraying her true nature would be unthinkable from that point on. Those who have undertaken such a quest or a similar initiation come away with a new understanding of their life purpose".*

Caroline also states *"that Visionaries are often outsiders, and who in their youth, felt like they just didn't fit in. That as difficult and lonely as that might have been, this shaped you into the Visionary you were to become."* I recognised these aspects of the Visionary in myself, since that first recognition as a child of the artist within.

The Visionary worked alongside the Rebel of my youth; I was a loner and disruptor. The Visionary was also present during my Innocent years of child-rearing and building my future with them. A force of inspiration as a business owner (it's pretty hard to build a business without vision!) But the Visionary and the Creator combined? These two Archetypes were not dualities; in fact, they are almost the same, complementary and highly effectual.

I feel that I should point out that the process and research of the Archetypes and their meaning was the primary factor in their creation (the paintings). The analysis and linking them to my life came afterwards when I had finished them. It was only after the complete series had landed on the canvas, that I was able to decipher the meaning behind what I had made. The stories I have told of my mother and father are important,

[3] Caroline Myss, Archetypes who are you? Hay House Inc., copyright 2013. Carlsbad CA.

as I believe that to know who we are, we also need to know where we come from, and what influences were responsible for that outcome. In an Archetypal sense, they set up the dichotomy for the remainder of the series. They are the juxtaposed aspects of dark and light, good and bad, the paternal and maternal face-off against each other. The Ruler and Creator referenced my career, the middle ground of my life. The Ruler was my past career, and the Creator was my current and future career.

If the *Creator* is my current outer armour and projects what I do in the world, then the *Visionary* is my inner Archetype, that invisible authentic aspect that is my soul. We can also evolve through the Archetypal system or patterns as our roles in life change; however, this also depends upon a personal open willingness to embrace change or the want to evolve. Perhaps this is part of the process of being human, and we need to experience ourselves in many guises, occupations and life situations. In my view, most humans are too rigid in their beliefs, or social conditioning to want to step outside their comfort zones. Whilst I am not trying to advocate a right or wrong, these are my personal findings; which I have chosen to share in the hope that they may also inspire people to explore aspects of themselves they have privately hidden for fear of ridicule or possibly even failure (heaven forbid!)

For the *Visionary* Archetype, (according to Jung scripture) the vision quest is a rebirth; therefore it seemed only apt that the Visionary should be portrayed in a very natural and mortal state, emerging from the darkness, reborn to a new life. This was the hessian hood I created to photograph myself in, for reference to make the other paintings from. I may not have had any sort of shaman initiation, but my art practice and the investigation from my soul's perspective, certainly awakened and directed my new career path as an artist - the *Creator*. This was my final painting in the series (the end), yet it could also read as the first one (a beginning). I am the raw emerging artist, birthing from the baptism of the dark waters, and ready for my next life.

At the summation of *The Immortal Soul*, I proudly presented the paintings, accompanied with a thesis and awaited judgement for my Bachelor of Visual Art. I was awarded a Pass! Considering the grades were High Distinction, Distinction, Credit, Pass, Fail; being awarded a Pass mark, felt like a massive FAIL! I had put my heart and soul into this work, it was my personal *Frida Kahlo*, my *Piéce De Résistance*, my tribute to *Carl Jung*, and an understanding of my life, exposed on canvas for all to see and judge. I was totally gutted. But I also didn't care! The Rebel in me acknowledged that I had done my own thing. I had not conformed to their (art school's) ideal of what they expected from their students. The reasoning behind my low mark was in not delivering a body of work that was more captivating and engaging to a broader audience. In other words, it was too personal and private.

But I beg to differ on that judgment because artists throughout time have used their own lives as subject matter for inspiration. Frida Kahlo is a prime example, by utilising her pain to express herself on canvas, which further emboldened her to decorate her own body as a work of living art through her fashion statements. A great majority of her paintings are self-portraits. Vincent Van Gogh's self-portrait with bandaged ear absolutely defined him, and also immortalized his pain.

I also feel that it's OK to fail at things, and reflect on my previous degree; a Bachelor of Visual Communication, which led to my previous career as a graphic designer. I failed one project in my final year - which was a wine label design! So, when a *real* job presented itself - a pitch for a wine label concept in the *real* world, I gave it my all, to prove to myself what I was capable of. And the rest, as they say, is history!

Chapter 5

Let's go to Italy

IN BOCCA AL LUPO (into the wolf's mouth)

Enrolling in an art school in Italy was an excellent excuse to fulfil my love for travel, and to nurture my bruised artist's ego all at the same time. If I was so bad at this thing (art), then perhaps some tuition from the masters of Renaissance painting would be invaluable? And so I chose a six-week intensive course in painting and drawing at *The Florence Academy of Art*, right in the centre of Florence. And what better place to learn in, than the birthplace of the Renaissance era.

Going to live in a foreign country for six weeks was also reason enough for taking up Italian lessons. Even after fifteen years living with an Italian man, I still had not managed to master any of the Italian language, much to the dismay of his mother I might add. I thought it would be easy but soon realized that languages are just not my thing. I confess to being a bit lazy in that regard owing to having an Italian husband who was more than an adequate translator whilst travelling in that country. However, I didn't have that perk anymore either! One of the last phrases I learned from the Italian language class (which I did take with me) was *'in bocca al lupo'* which was important to know, as it is considered extremely bad luck to wish someone good luck in a literal way by saying *'buona fortuna.'* The lucky way to wish good fortune is to say *'in bocca al lupo,'* which translates as *'into the wolf's mouth'*. The equivalent English expression of *'break a leg.'* The *'in bocca al lupo'* metaphor compares any challenging scenario to being caught between the hungry jaws of a wild beast whose aim is to swallow both the misfortunate and the careless. The *'wolf'* can also be interpreted as *'your fears'*. A scenario of *'feel the fear and do it anyway'*.

In remembrance of who I was in my forties during a seminar on self-awareness and confidence building, the topic of *fear* was flagged. I think I was the only one who stated that I did not feel fear (of failure, for clarification). At that particular period in my life, I had a successful business, therefore my life felt secure and safe. So, what was there to fear? Exactly. But that was then. Twenty years on when the bravado of youth was no longer so present at my side, I realised that I was not in that place anymore. So, what had led me to this juncture in my life that made me choose a six-week intensive Renaissance drawing and painting course in Florence? FEAR! Fear that I would not be the best that I could possibly be. Fear that I may not ever sell a painting. Fear that my peers won't accept me in the art world. Yet I knew that my art was simply up to discipline, daily practice, exposure, and a willingness to turn up every day to my craft, and just do it. I was working on that bit!

Now I have to confess that another genuine fear of mine is the discomfort of travelling cattle-class when flying and all the unknowns that may reveal. Business-class, far more predictable, and once you've flown upfront it's pretty hard to go back. I don't care how many blockbuster movies you can watch back-to-back in one hit; the discomfort of sitting in an upright position whilst trying to sleep with screaming babies, people farting, and being trapped in a window seat with no escape from your comatose snoring companion is enough to create a genuine phobia - *the FEAR of flying!* But yet, it was still not enough to deter me, and a mere twenty-four-hour journey was worth the disruption. To be thrust into another culture on the opposite side of the world, to hone my craft, for me was the inspiration I sought which would help to validate my artist's journey. The idea of an adventure and the unknown was also pretty exciting, even though I had been to Italy many times before.

This adventure, however, turned out to be a case of *seemed like a good idea at the time!* And from the time I disembarked from the plane in Venice, I began to feel that I had made a great big fat mistake! I questioned my reasoning behind it and everything I came up with was unjustifiable and in fact, could only be explained as a *deliberate disruption* to my life. For some odd reason, I decided to fly into Venice simply because I knew it well. I then caught a train to Florence, which was an easy and pleasant Vaporetto ride from the airport to the train station. But after the 24-hour plane journey, a rocking train is a great panacea for sleep, which I fought off owing to the fear of falling into a coma and ending up in Roma.

From the time I had booked to the time I paid, the bottom had fallen out of the Aussie dollar and it was costing me much more than I originally budgeted for. I had a very comfortable home and lifestyle. The last week at home had been typically glorious South Australian sunny spring days in the low twenties accompanied by azure diamond blue skies the likes of which you can only find in the land of Oz. As I had fluttered around my house with its newly renovated kitchen and new French doors to the studio, I had felt that I was putting the finishing touches onto a painting. I had wallowed and basked in the beauty of my environment, my home of two years since the demise of my second marriage. I was happy here, I felt safe and financially secure.

As I disembarked from the train station on the last leg of the journey, my fear turned into sheer panic, and I began questioning the motive behind my seemingly (now) ridiculous decision to study an art course in Italy. All for a disruption! But I hadn't gone to Antarctica; I'd chosen Florence – not exactly the arse end of the earth, was it? Six weeks at the Academia of Art learning the atelier style of true Renaissance drawing and painting, Bellissima! What was wrong with me? Perhaps, just perhaps, I had grown up at last and needed to settle down with my comforts and appreciate the life I had made for myself? I started to question EVERYTHING I was doing. After a walk through the darkening evening, from the train station in Florence, with map in hand, I finally found my home-to-be for the next six weeks; an Air B&B apartment, which was a very basic bolt hole with a tiny balcony. This overlooked a rather untidy back alley and a noisy schoolyard. It was old and rustic and I won't build it into something it wasn't, because it was a far cry from what I was used to, put it that way. A room no larger than three by four metres with a mezzanine bedroom loft I accessed via a ladder. The bedroom consisted of a mattress on the mezzanine floor. There was no kitchen. The plan was to eat out, and face that social fear I have of eating alone, by forcing myself to just go out and meet people. There it was again, FEAR! I had chosen the B&B based on the name of the district (Santo Spirito) and the fact it was located on the other side of the Arno River and required a good three-kilometre walk every day across the Ponte Vecchio bridge to the Academy, every morning and afternoon. I also liked the fact it was owned by an artist and adorned with eclectic original artwork. But let's face it, most Air B&B pictures look far more enticing on the website than in physical actuality. Ironically when I stepped into the apartment I was greeted by a painting of a wolf, running, and mouth wide open as well. I smiled and thought to myself, *'well of course, what else should I expect but a visual reminder of the truth.'*

Quite possibly my greatest fear is that of being alone. My art sustains me and also gives me an obscene amount of inner dialogue. Artists are renowned for mining their lives for material, and even periodically setting dynamite to it - if only to shake things up a bit. I had deliberately created this disruption, so why was I so terribly homesick, and from the first day I arrived, I might add? I missed my house, my king-sized bed, the brand-new kitchen, fresh smoothies from the Nutri-Bullet in the mornings, sun streaming through the north-facing French doors, and then the west setting sun late in the day through the studio doors. I missed my newly made art friends, and I missed more than anything my great big fat panther of a black cat, Galiano. I was aware that the trip may do just this; give me a greater sense of appreciation for what I already had. And that is absolutely fine, isn't it? But deep in the recesses of my psyche, in the dark corners hiding, - was love. It had been two years since I had left my husband. Did I feel like there was some sort of answer to the question my dream had posed, by visiting the scene of the crime? The place where we'd honeymooned? I went to the St Lorenzo Cathedral many times during my six-week stay - I didn't know what I was looking for - but yes, I did; I wanted to fall truly, madly, deeply in love - one more time, please, just once more, I promise I'll stay!

In the words of the Rolling Stones song, *'you don't always get what you want. Sometimes, you get what you need…'* never had a truer word been sung. Now the first week at the Academy had been a bit like Chinese torture to be quite honest. Walking three kilometres to and from the school every day (that's six kilometres in total) and then adjusting to standing for seven hours in front of an easel to learn the pain-staking ancient task of the true atelier drawing technique was, well, bloody boring! We worked on copy drawings in the style of Charles Bargue[4] exacting the mastery of *how to draw* with silverpoint, charcoal sticks and pencil. This exacting and painful process endured for four of the six weeks before we proceeded to draw from live models, and then finally, experiment with paint in the last week. We were taught the process of painting a portrait and was the only class I actually enjoyed! I understand the need to be able to draw and paint well, in fact even Vincent Van Gogh had completed the entire set of Bargue drawings *twice* during his lifetime before he felt inclined to *break the rules*. Perhaps this is what drove him mad! And we know that the great Picasso painted like a realist pro until he awoke at age 21 and began to paint with the wild abandon of a child. The course made me realise that my skill base was already pretty solid. What I did learn from the six-week intensive drawing and painting course was patience, primarily with the art of making – this takes time, and patience with myself - to stop being so hard and critical about my decisions, and my life in general. I needed to go with the flow more, and trust that everything had a purpose, every decision had an effect and I needed to exercise patience with that critical aspect of myself.

There was a share house, which had been offered through the course for attending students and apparently, this was a gorgeous Florentine apartment with five bedrooms. Most of the younger students had opted for this accommodation. Located just around the corner from the Academy they would go home for lunch, and return with the conviviality that only friendship procures. Why, oh why, had I chosen to be Ms Independent with a place of my own! A lesson in hindsight, it would have been a far more

---

[4] The Charles Bargue Drawing Course is the collected set of knowledge from centuries of academic art education. It is being used in classical art academies throughout the world. It was developed and widely used in the mid-19th century as a foundational exercise for fine art training. Since the comeback of traditional values art schools and academies have been formed which follow this proven approach of the great masters. This approach is an essential process in understanding the principles of shape, proportion, value and form.

enriching experience and I would have established friendships throughout my six-week tenure. Instead, my duration in Florence was a lonely time of deep reflection on the past, and an opportunity to contemplate my future. It was here, where I had come to learn the tools of the Renaissance painters, coupled with the hope of finding love again (who doesn't want a little holiday romance), in my bolt-hole, the wolf breathing down my back, and feeling utter crushing loneliness, that I began writing this book. Unbeknownst to me at the time, it was a gathering of thoughts, which became a jigsaw puzzle I later collated into this title. Perhaps my creative juices were not satiated enough at the school with the tedious task of mere mark-making, and these found their way onto the page as words?

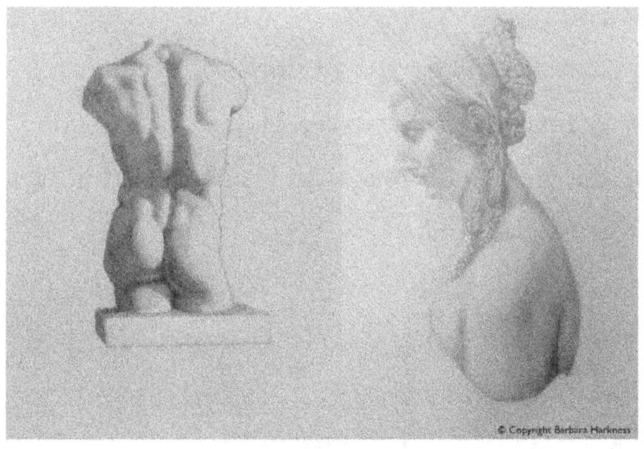

Charles Bargue copy drawing

drawing created from a statue
Palazzo Strozzi - Florence

My plans for eating out in the evening were thwarted by rather rude waiters who tried to persuade me into having three courses rather than simply one (which is all I wanted). Post the GFC; much of Italy had suffered through the lack of tourists spending their moolah as generously as they had, so the establishment would tack on a rather large gratuity surcharge, which was not divulged before ordering. I would always question what this charge pertained to, only to be responded to with angry raised voices and lots of hand gestures. I figured it was just a general *'pissed off, we don't like you English anyway'* fee, and covered their annoyance at having to deal with the tourists. Well, that's what it felt like, and so I stopped going out for dinner and would instead swing by the supermarket for some antipasto and a bottle of wine, then I'd sit and write. I went within, it was healing and cathartic.

I exited Italy the same way I came in, via Venice. This was my fifth visit to the beautiful sinking city, which holds a certain fascination for most people; mainly an engineering accomplishment, but probably for me, it was the romantic vibe and my past link with it. The Venice Biennale was also on this year (2015), which was the major reason for my short stay after the art course had finished.

There is a bar in Venice called Harry's Bar, made famous for its Bellini's. It is the icon of all places to visit for a drink or a feed, and a must on any tourist's agenda.

I noticed it quite accidentally upon my arrival at the Hotel Flora, as I turned the corner onto the Calle Vaporesso, and thought to myself *'oh there's Harry's Bar, maybe I shall finally get to have a drink there'*. Previously and during our second visit to Venice, my husband and I had walked for what seemed hours trying to find Harry's Bar. It seemed as elusive and repetitive as the alleyways Venice offered up. When we finally found it, we sat down and ordered a bottle of water, received the menu and to our horror realised that a decent feed was probably going to cost in the vicinity of AU$250! We'd looked around to the other stunned tourists who sadly looked like they had also been lured into a trap and were now captured. Promptly we'd decided to escape while we could, paying 18 euros for the sparkling water and left.

Returning to the hotel one evening I simply happened upon Harry's again and found a group of English tourists outside debating the horror of something? I assumed it must be the prices, but they had apparently been refused entry, owing to one fellow's attire of long shorts, or perhaps they were short longs – either way, the owners of the restaurant had decided that they were not suitable enough for entering their restaurant to dine in. They were otherwise very smartly dressed, except for the long-shorts fellow! That evening as I wandered the alleyways trying to find an establishment to eat at, I decided to treat myself to a meal at Harry's Bar. I knew it would be expensive, but this would probably be my last time in Italy. I don't need to come back here again.

But what to wear? I had one pair of heels with me but didn't really feel like donning the only dress I brought with me (that just in case little black number), so I teamed the high heels with a pair of jeans and my super cool black leather *Goddess of Babylon* jacket (plug for the brand). This jacket I take with me everywhere, because it's made from super-thin leather and therefore packs very well. Embellished with little gold studs and hand-embroidered with criss-cross black leather trim, I love it because of its artistry, therefore I always feel great when I wear it. That's my basic philosophy with clothes in a nutshell, buy well, and buy less. But, would I get in with my strategically ripped - holey moley - faded and jaded - well-worn - and now slightly painted, jeans? The rebel in me could not resist the challenge!

"Would madam like a table for one", the concierge asked as I entered the restaurant, with no resistance I might add.

"Yes, it's just me", I replied.

Phew, I was in. Elated that I was let into the joint, I settled in and observed the crowd around me. There were lots of Americans and Aussies, and it was noisy with conversation. As I sat there on my own, I realised that I had come to accept being on my own and overcome *that* fear! I ordered the famous Bellini and four chicken croquet snacks (which was all I could afford), I reflected on my journey, and my last night in Italy.

Isn't it interesting, that sometimes in life the more we search, the less likely we are to find that which we are searching for? When, if you relax, it is usually just around the corner and you simply stumble upon it. This journey, a return to romantic places from the past had made me realise that sometimes going from point A to point B and revisiting the past, is like being allowed to encounter the tracks of our former selves, and to see how much we have grown. Upon my leaving the bar that evening, an Italian couple arrived in their jeans, puffer jackets and sneakers, who were also refused entry because of their attire. They were disappointed; perhaps they had come to Venice and spent hours trying to find it as we had. So, I caught up to them and spoke in English. I told them that they had just saved themselves a lot of money, but they looked at my jeans and we all laughed very hard. I was not sure if they understood my English, because they were very Italian, but they did understand the parody of the situation.

When I arrived back in Australia and entered my home, I got down on my knees and kissed the ground. It was so good to be home, Toto!

Chapter 6

And let's just stay home

"The only journey worth taking - is the journey within."
– William Butler Yeats

Whilst I was in Florence a girlfriend, Billie, had minded the house and Galiano. I had also previously rented the house to Billie and her two children when she felt the desperate need to leave her husband, and so she felt a special affiliation with it because she had lived here for two years. The house held special memories for Billie, because of *her* personal journey,.

Billie had candidly said to me on one occasion "Barbara, this is not your house you know, it's just on loan to you, and it will become someone else's house when you die – or sell it."

"I know that Bills and you are most welcome to own it with me, whilst I am in residence, and also in my absence."

Since her stage 4 cancer diagnosis Billie had packed up her life in preparation for her pending death and gone to live in Sydney with her twin sister. She had one daughter in Sydney and one here in Adelaide. My home became her refuge during her illness, whenever she came to Adelaide. She loved my house as I did. My home had a wonderful vibe, which many people connected with. I was only too happy to share it with her, now more so than ever, on her journey towards the inevitable.

Strangely, we never talked about *'it'*. Until, on one of the stays, when I opened the front door to her, she had this huge smile on her face, and I knew.

"It's finally happening isn't it," I said.

"Yes, they have done all they can, if they cut any more of me away, there won't be anything left!"

"How long?" I asked out of curiosity.

"Don't know, don't care," and we left it at that.

I digress! Whilst I was away in Italy and Billie was minding the house another tumour appeared, which required immediate surgery and a short stint in hospital. She took all of the cancer removal surgery as if it were quite simply part of her life now, just another procedure – but ever so grateful to have another day. Which was why she never wanted to talk about it. Billie was very candid about her condition and could make light of it, rather than wallow in self-pity. She arrived back at the house from the hospital on the same day I got back from Florence. I was relieved to have her company and to care for her during her recovery. She was not allowed to travel for four weeks after the operation, owing to the intensity of the operation (one-third of her lung had been removed, owing to the metastasized cancer). I seized the opportunity to cook good healthy, wholesome food to share. My body was craving vegetables and freshly made juices after the pasta, pizza and pastries I had been eating for the last six weeks. I don't know what it is about tourist destinations, but it seemed terribly hard to find good healthy food!

Having a kitchen again was bliss and an invalid guest even more reason to cook up a storm of vegan delights. My favourite recipe of Indian Kitchari, a restorative meal given to recovering mothers after giving birth, was given a real workout. It was laborious to make but worth the effort as we ate it every day for the first week.

I had experienced utter crushing loneliness in Florence on a scale I had not ever experienced in my life before. I came back to my convalescing friend who was living in my home. Before the week was out, I received an email from my eldest son who also wanted to come home for a short stay, which turned into six months!

The Inn was full: there were loads of washing to do, meals to prepare, food to be bought, movies to be watched, TV series to binge on, visitors and strangers constantly flowed in and out to visit Billie. Suddenly I had a full house and was loving every single minute and detail of the days! It was at this point that I realised my journey to Florence was about just this; appreciation for what I already have, amplified one hundred-fold upon my return, coupled with a greater sense of appreciation for the people in my life; my family and friends.

Had I stayed in the sharehouse with all the younger artists at the Academy I quite possibly would have wanted my space back, for the solitude? Even though the sharehouse was absolutely gorgeous and spacious, being the age I was (and used to my own home) I'd opted for an apartment of my own. Was this a mistake? Yes. But it was also *not* a mistake; the experience was just simply different because of this choice. Next time, I go with the flow and take what is on offer, rather than control the situation. Something had shifted within me and I felt it acutely. I was more relaxed about the flow in life and I was in awe of how easy everything became, I had more clarity about myself, my art, and creating a future exhibition, I had ideas, and I finally felt *unblocked*.

Nothing fazed me; there was chatter and conversation because Billie spent extraordinary lengths of time on her phone nurturing her multitudes of friendships, otherwise called gossiping! We all pitched in with meals, washing up, gardening and whatever else needed attending in the home. My painting studio was now my son's bedroom, but I managed to move my easel and paints into half of the room, thereby allowing room for the blow-up bed and the usual spread of clothes, books and laptops. More relevant, there was laughter, there was company, and there was certainly no more loneliness. I was grateful to have my son back and for the opportunity to heal our relationship, which only time could. It had been twenty years since I left the marriage, but he still bore the wounds of my departure. A mother's guilt, damn, does it ever dissipate?

A week after he arrived, he secured a contract with Rising Sun Productions, a Hollywood blockbuster post-production company, doing what he does so well, compositing the movie scenes. Simple things like being side by side with him in the kitchen whilst I prepared breakfast and he made his salad for work, then watching him walk out the door and say, *"Bye, mum, see you tonight"* was like reliving a parallel life.

I had left the marriage when he was seventeen years old, thinking that they needed their father more than their mother in their teenage years and that they would both be OK. I realised now that these were formative years when a young man learns patterns of behaviour, such as how to interact with a woman, how to cook, how to be polite, to understand the feminine, to respect women, when to take on the big jobs, finding the masculine alongside the feminine, and how the two intertwine. He had not known what a healthy relationship looked or felt like, owing to my absence and therefore not been shown the way. I hoped that this time with me would mend some of those missing links to his life and the chinks in his armour. The laws of magnetic karma had brought us together again, in the most important relationship given - that of our blood ties. He came from my womb - he was my flesh and blood. Of course, that invisible umbilical cord was still there, complete with a great big knot right in the middle. Perhaps these magnetic forces are far more powerful, and more necessary when children are involved. I felt powers beyond my control at work here and became acutely aware that this was Daniel's and my time.

He got to witness how I interacted with others, he saw us having fun and came along to everything we invited him to; markets, art gallery events, movie nights. He wanted to belong and so into the women's fold he was gathered.

Billie eventually left when she was able to travel back to Sydney. Daniel vacated the studio to take the guest room, enabling me to write and paint once more in peaceful bliss. But not before a morning convene in the kitchen over poached eggs with spinach and avocado, sometimes it was just a rushed bowl of muesli. But I made sure that I was there for breakfast, otherwise, I would have missed him for the day.

On Daniel's first day on the new job, he arose early and made his uber-healthy salad lunch for work. As he bounded out the door to start the 1.5 km walk into town, I said, *"don't forget your hat"*, and felt the impulse to give him a big hug. He was only going to work! But I did it all the same, and possibly because I felt that I had not done this enough when he was a young boy. I savoured every waking moment he was in my home. I made sure I was present in every moment so that I could enjoy my son, as I never had before. He stepped over that doorstep and through the gate, throwing back a smile to me. This simple act of being, doing, and belonging, between us, was the healing power of love doing its work.

As I watched my grown-up, thirty-seven-year-old handsome young man go off to work, I also saw my five-year-old going to school. Every day he spent with me replaced my years of neglect. I know that I could never make up for those years (or the pain) but my conscience told me that we'd both been given this wonderful opportunity to repair the past, and I was going to make sure I did a damned good job at being a mother to him whilst he around.

Sometimes we are lucky enough to have a second chance in life, or should I say life situations. We very rarely get a second chance at love. I was extremely pleased that this time he got to leave me, and not the other way around. I knew that my leaving had hurt and scarred him deeply, but this short-lived opportunity to share our lives again delivered a sense of repair. He taught me a lot too, to just go with the flow and trust the universe with what we already know. That we are looked after, and when we connect with our true nature, then amazing things happen. Our deepest desires are revealed to us in uncanny, unexpected and delightful surprises of serendipity and chance.

"Trust your instincts and always follow your heart," I wrote to him in a card when he finally departed. He was going to India for three months to study the practice of Yoga in an Ashram, not his usual line of work, but something he had promised himself he would do – one day. I gave blessings of gratitude for all that I had in my life when he left, and cried all the way home from the airport, back to my empty house and life of solitude.

From the great Morgan Freeman; who says... "If someone prays for patience does God give them patience...or does he allow them the opportunity to develop patience? If you pray for courage, does he instantly bestow courage upon you, ... or provide the situation, which requires courage to show up? If someone prayed for the family to be closer, does he provide an opportunity that facilitates this?"

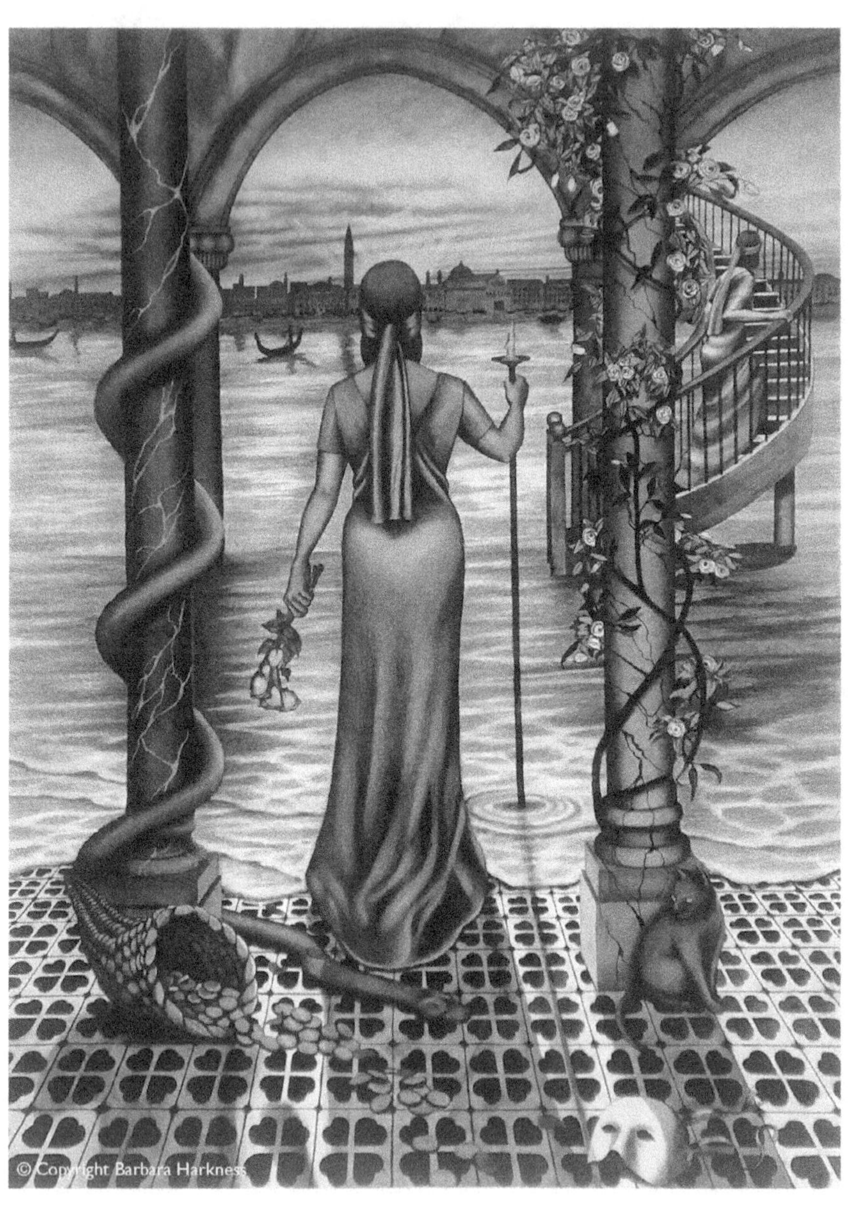

The Magician
charcoal sketch

Chapter 7

The Magician

"Have no fear of perfection - you'll never reach it!"

- Salvador Dali

Full of inspiration and crazy ambition after my Italian Renaissance sojourn, I decided to paint onto a REALLY BIG canvas - as the Renaissance painters did. I thought that I was ready for the task - but I wasn't. No big deal, hindsight is a wonderful thing – in hindsight! I had allocated to myself, the luxurious time frame of a year in which to complete a painting. After all, I had learnt the art of patience from the Academy and during my fact-finding mission to Florence I had discovered that the great Renaissance painters often took many years to complete their works of art (they also had apprentices – which I didn't!) And so this was how I planned to work for a whole year, on one very solid and dedicated project.

I had received a vision during an art history class on the Renaissance period, whilst I was at art school. At the time I had quickly sketched this onto my pad during the coffee break, then once home, did another sketch with more detail. I kept expanding upon the sketch until I finally had the vision clearly articulated with all the fine detail I required, which I worked up into a charcoal drawing, in the same way that Anna Platten does. I even went to great lengths and had a red silk dress personally made, followed by a photo shoot on the beach at sunset, complete with a broom handle as my prop, for the required photographic reference in the painting.

At the start of the project, I had the wonderful benefit of receiving a psychic reading of the painting, by a friend. Milica was a Reiki Master and a natural intuitive. I had met her through my friend Billie, (who had finally passed away from her cancer) so when she entered the house; she asked if she could go to the guest room (Billie's bedroom). Both Milica and Billie were second-generation children of Serbian refugees. Milica was also the person who informed me when Billie had passed. Needless to say, through these circumstances, we had developed a connection. But I was not expecting her reaction when she went through to the studio and saw the painting on my easel in the studio.

She gasped and cried out "oh my God, I've got goosebumps all over!"

I had not displayed the painting to many people yet, because it was also only in the developmental stages of presenting as an under-painting. But the essence and structure were in place and therefore the narrative could be read.

"Can I do a reading on it, Barbara? It's so powerful."

"Absolutely, I'd love to hear your interpretation Milica."

Considering she only knew me through our mutual friend, I was fascinated to know what she could interpret intuitively from my painting, about my life, and me for that matter.

This is a transcript of her reading.

"This lifetime is our castle, in which we imprison ourselves to an extent. Not often do we venture out into life to experience what we are really capable of. To me now, this woman is finally able to summon the courage to step outside the castle and the protection barrier she has built around her. She is still a little scared, but she wants more than she has given herself.

The repetition of the tiles, and the heart pattern, speaks of the patterns we repeat in life. In particular, the heart speaks of the soul. You are done with this physical world, and the repetitive nature of the journey in this lifetime. Look at them; you have even created a four-leaf clover pattern, which indicates you have made your own luck in life. You know how to manifest through the art of creating.

The discarded mask represents breaking out of that archetypal pattern as well. Removing the mask, barriers and limitations that are self-imposed. Now it is time for your raw truth to be exposed, without masks, without restraint.

The cat represents nine lives in a superstitious sense, and she has survived many lives as well.

The snake represents a protector and also the shedding aspect. The snake is a powerful animal guide, a symbol of transformation and wisdom expressed through healing. She is ready to shed because she finally has the courage.

The stairway is the ascension process. This represents the beginning of her new life. The water represents the soul, our depth, and the fact that this stairwell comes out from the water means that she is finished with this superficial building on the earth plane and is now seeking something higher, a more meaningful existence. She has experienced all there is on the earth plane, and there are only so many times you can keep repeating the same pattern over and over, then what do you do after that?"

"Oh, thanks for clarifying the staircase, because it had confused me. I thought it might have been a detour because I am faced directly straight ahead, but this stairwell is off to the side?" I was painting from a vision, which I had responded to without bias or analysis.

"No, because it ascends from the water which represents spirituality, you are simply seeking. And look at you curiously peering to see what is around the corner, it's so obvious, Barbara. You are searching for something, and it's not far away".

I then explained to her how the sunrise will create a glow around my head because of the positioning, and how challenging this was going to be without it looking like I am some sort of religious saint. This was purely incidental, that the rising sun of the brand-new day coincided with the placement of my head.

"Well, that's what you are seeking, isn't it? Enlightenment. So perhaps during the process of painting this vision, you will attain enlightenment also?"

I liked her take on things, especially seeing her reaction. Moreso, I respected her psychic intuition.

I referenced my mentor (Anna Platten) and working in the same way she did, created a finely detailed charcoal sketch for the painting, and then projected it onto the canvas. My Renaissance painting developed many titles; the first being *'The Goddess returns,'* then *'I am, therefore, I was and shall be,'* which is pretty grandiose, I know! Upon its completion, I realized I had painted a giant Tarot card and therefore ended up calling it *'The Magician.'* In matching up similar traits, I found the first Major Arcana Card *'The Magician'* aligned with my painting. *The Magician* is considered an alchemical worker, and is depicted with one arm pointing toward the ground and the other arm pointing to the sky, evoking the axiom *'as above, so below'*. *'The Magician'* card includes the four symbols of the Tarot suits; a cup, pentacle, sword and wand, with each symbolising one of the four elements; water, earth, air and fire. These are signs that he has all the tools (and elements) he needs to manifest his intentions into being. There is usually an array of foliage and flowers, symbolising the blossoming and fruition of ideas and aspirations on the card. My painting has most of these characteristics, and elements, however the primary link to that of '*The Magician*' is the wand that I hold in my right hand. The pentacles of course are the coins lying on the ground. Even though all reference to '*The Magician*' in Tarot is male, he is always clothed in a red cloak, I related to this aspect even more so, owing to my strong sense of the animus[5]. *The Magician* is all about will and the nature of change and the question, '*which is more important: the tools you have set before you, or the will to change?*'

[5] Jung described the animus as the unconscious masculine side of a woman, and the anima as the unconscious feminine side of a man, each transcending the personal psyche.

Chapter 8

If that's all there is, then let's keep dancing

"If the song in my heart ceases to play,
can I survive in the silence"
- Shonda Rhimes

I met him at the Gaslight Tavern, a grungy little pub where musos from all walks of life gathered to improvise their pure blues music. Music aficionados would listen and dance enthusiasts would strut their stuff on the tiny dance floor. It was different every time depending on the crowd and who was playing. Now and then a famous musician would pop in to play, (I'm told) so that they could feel like a regular person again, in the cramped living room atmosphere with *the family* of other musos. At times it was packed with old men, resembling a Vietnam War Vets convention, and other times it convulsed with women in strappy dresses and high heels dancing provocatively to the bluesy tunes.

Mario danced like no one was watching, but everyone was and he knew it. He made vertical love on the dance floor with his infamous 'dips' and grinding hips. The women squealed and laughed when he dipped them so low he swept the floor with their hair. There were no special steps, no rules, just Mario's style; like the club itself, improvised and sexy! I couldn't take my eyes off him, mesmerised by this man, whose dance card was absolutely full. Then one night, to my surprise he took to the stage with the band. And I thought, *'wow this gets better'*, and sure enough, the man had a brilliant voice as well, a cross between Tony Bennett and Dean Martin. He was an ultimate entertainer and loved the limelight. Not only were women drawn to him, but men too.

He gave everyone his time, making sure he hugged and kissed them all. Mario was a magnet and I was drawn to him like a moth to a flame, and from there on, he had me at *'hello'* every time I walked into the joint.

I found myself recommissioning my red suede mini skirt, which I had relegated to the dress-up box, but drew the line at high heels (too hard to dance in)! The instinct to wear dresses instead of jeans kicked in like a newly born foal, and before I knew it - I was making vertical love on the dance floor with Mario too. Not ever having had a dance partner in my life, I was used to leading (mainly because not many men know how to dance). With Mario, I leaned in, let go, and started to enjoy the debut, of what would become the Barrio floor show.

The Gaslight Tavern was the slow burn to the start of our relationship, he eventually asked me out on a date, two days before New Years eve 2016, which was about a year after I first met him. I'm not so sure he expected me to accept, as he seemed surprised when I said yes. Mario took me to a Maltese Ball for New Year, which is an event held in a community hall. The average age is around seventy, the round tables surrounding the walls allow for maximum dance space, the food is ordinary (a kind way of saying awful) and the band suited the occasion and the demographic (ethnic). Mario liked these events because he usually got asked to sing, therefore raising the bar, and getting the applause he so loved. All who knew him always welcomed having Mario belt out a tune at an event, with warm enthusiasm.

Having not been asked out on a date in this fashion for over four years, I was ecstatic (plus I was keen on the guy). Being as it was a ball, I frocked up in the 1957 vintage vogue red satin dress I had made for my fiftieth birthday, complete with a stiff red petticoat for good old fashioned effect. I could tell that he was quite pleased I had made the effort and had the right attitude towards a simple New Years Eve for oldies.

As we walked in arm in arm, he said to me "you do know we are going to have to make our own fun here?"

"Of course" I replied, "I've got this." I was just so pleased with finally being asked out!

We danced all night, and even received the *'best dance couple'* award at the nights end!

My New Years resolution was to say "YES" to everything. Mario asked me out and everything in my life seemed to take on a positive flow as a result of saying "YES". This was an experiment, and a positive one I must add because many of the things I experienced with him I would have previously rejected. My prejudgement would have deemed them (being a snob here) not up to my usual standard. I had so much fun, being in these new circumstances. I didn't have to embrace them completely, however surrendering to the flow allowed for enjoying the moment for what it was, and more often than not, *it* was hilarious!

There is a side effect to getting a boyfriend at last. You generate simple acts of kindness in the effort to impress that person, and before you know it, there are deeper feelings. And so I asked him one day, "would you like to be written into my life script?"

"Of course I would!" he replied.

"Just for clarity then, when were you thinking of pegging out?"

"Possibly around Seventy five, I think that would be considered a good inning for me."

"Great, that works in with my nine-year cycle perfectly" (he was at the time sixty-six).

"What if I don't peg out?"

"Well, I might have to renegotiate that when and if the time arrives."

Too much futurising, we both agreed. I had inadvertently written him into my script anyway, and what was working for us both, was a lack of expectation of the other. We were a couple, I enjoyed being his girlfriend, and he enjoyed being my boyfriend. It was a playful way of looking at life in our mature years, as we simply enjoyed going out to gigs and shows, dancing and mingling with other people. We were a good fit, and many people made the comment that we looked good together - as if we belonged. People who did not know us thought we were a married couple, owing to this fact, and they were surprised when we told them that we had been together for less than a year. That whole growing together melding effect, seemed to have arrived prematurely.

What worked so well for us was the fact there was *no expectation* of the other. I do believe that we were on the correct vibrational level for the sort of relationship we both needed. At the time, it was non-committal, based on trust and mutual respect.

Mario would stay over at my place on the weekends, we'd share the cooking and he would help with a few man chores. I was quite amused to find the karaoke gear inconspicuously installed into my studio one day. It just appeared (without my permission). But hey, this was my year of saying *'yes'* to everything, and so I didn't question it. Instead, I found myself trying to sing, but ultimately finding my feet instead. My art studio became a dance studio on the weekends - it was large and had a wonderful wooden parquetry floor to practise on. We perfected the aerial yo-yo, travelling return, octopus, catapult and the under-arm sniff (all learned off YouTube). We then took our moves to the dance floor and delight of adoring fans. I'd never had a dance partner before, so this was a fabulously new experience for me. He was incredibly strong;

therefore trust was a must when he dipped me so low he made people gasp, (possibly thinking that he would never be able to return me to a vertical position). This caused complete strangers who had witnessed our dancing acrobatics, to comment, *"my god, I thought he was going to drop you, strangle you.... or both?"* and *"I'm glad someone knows what they're doing,"* which made me feel very privileged indeed! The fact that people cared enough to comment on our dancing spoke volumes to us both. Neither of us had ever taken any dance lessons, and when we told them so, they were even more astounded. When we first alighted to the dance floor we were both quite subdued, and then somewhere around the two-minute mark, I would feel a surge of adrenaline when our rhythm connected and we became one, each responding to knowing how the other moves and what to expect. Our dancing was *joyous*, never wanting to dance on my own ever again. This was the Barrio dance show, and we were whirling dervishes on fire.

After our first year together I reflected on our status and realised I had somehow gotten the things I'd asked for (subconsciously). I'd always wanted to go out with a musician, someone in a band in particular, so whilst he was not in a band, he played with other musicians often, so I got close. I wanted a partner who made me laugh, and we certainly kept each other amused with our light attitude on life. I also wanted a partner to dance with, and this is precisely where we out-performed in the relationship. Sometimes I think my mother's spirit had taken up residence in my legs because she had been a professional dancer and singer during WW11. I know she would have adored Mario for his Englebert Humperdink - Tom Jones stage presence and dancing prowess.

However, I had begun to question this whole *love* thing. I needed to get really clear on exactly what I wanted, and I have to confess I didn't actually know how to define what that looked like anymore (as a mature woman). Does it matter post sixty? So long as you are friends, are able-bodied, can laugh at things, including yourself? Surely this is as good as it gets? But, I found myself wanting more.

When *the want* silently crept in, it settled down beside me and became my constant shadow. What is it about human nature that constantly *wants* for more? Till the day I leave this earthly existence, I will question everything, especially myself.

Looking back over my life and the patterns I had created along the way, (and wanted no more of) brought up a few simple truths. I was running the show again, creating and organising the relationship, and it didn't sit well with me. Expectation crept in, from both of us. He wanted me to attend his family affairs, and I didn't want to. He wanted me to attend all of his gigs, and I didn't want to go to the same ones over and over. The relationship always happened at my place, because I had a more convivial environment. He lived in a share house with his brother and son, and there were always a few ring-ins as well, so privacy was compromised. This started to become mundane and I looked forward to his eventual leaving on Sunday night at the end of the weekend. A year after we began our relationship, and over the Xmas period, he landed on Xmas Eve and left on New Year's Day. A whole weeks holiday for him at the Harkness Hilton! At first, it didn't bother me, I was still in *yes* mode. But when I did not get *any* acknowledgement on New Year's Eve (our 1st anniversary) at the very least for my work as an extraordinary hostess with the mostess, let alone being his girlfriend, I let it be known that I was *not happy!* I realised that expectation had set in, and like any normal woman, I wanted my bunch of *fucking-thank-you* flowers!

His reply "well what do I get in return?"

"You get me!"

"Well if you want our relationship to be defined by societal expectations, then you have the wrong guy" he curtly replied.

I pondered that statement and realised that I was just plain disappointed at not being acknowledged for the '*girlfriend of the year*' award, having tried so hard to impress him. And so I started to set a few boundaries. I also acknowledged (to myself) that if I was relieved when he finally left on Sunday night after the weekends then I was never going to ask him to stay for the rest of my life. The patterns were repeating, and I felt I was slipping back into an existence of being taken for granted once more, just like I had been in my marriage. 2018 became my *maybe* year! I pulled back and did not relinquish *yes* to everything on the table. I had enjoyed my year of *yes*, don't get me wrong, but in doing so, I had surrendered my life to someone else once again. I would have to say from that moment on, it was downhill. We tried to stay on the same plane we had been flying together, but unfortunately, that had crashed.

The human expectation of wanting more! See how fragile our psyches are, because of our own self-imposed societal conditioning. I let it go - but I didn't. Deep inside, I wanted my homely acts of kindness to be acknowledged, I wanted my generosity of food and shelter on the weekend, to be appreciated, I wanted my temple (my body), to be worshipped, and I wanted the love I gave, to be acknowledged. The human expectation was to blame of course, and so it came to pass that we got right out of sync, and in time so did our dancing. One night at our favourite dance venue, he simply said to me "are you ok, you're not letting me lead?"

"Well in fact Mario, I have been letting you lead and yes, we are out of sync." He knew what I meant.

So when my son Daniel came to stay again (for work purposes), I used this as the perfect opportunity to push him away. No more staying over on the weekend, sorry, I have another man in my life and being my son, he has automatic priority. This was six months after the new years incident, but the festering sore was there because I'd simply applied a band-aid. It was interesting to see how easy it was to choose *not to love* someone. I had flicked that switch off, my choice. Or how, where energy goes, things flow - or not. My energy was now directed into my relationship with my son. I believed that he had come back into my life for a reason; a magnetic pairing of individual personal needs attracted the situation. Daniel was stuck in Sydney in his apartment, having gutted the kitchen, and unable to move ahead with his renovations owing to the body corporate laws and an insurance claim. He was sleeping on the floor on a mattress, his only furniture, with no other creature comforts. So, when his work contract finished, he decided that Adelaide was a good option, where mother's home had a spare bedroom and a guest bathroom, and good home-style vegan meals. I relished every opportunity to enjoy my time with Daniel, and during that time I let my relationship with Mario go. Priority? Yes! Excuse? Absolutely! Six weeks turned into three months.

We all have choices; every day we choose what to eat, what to wear, how to project ourselves in the world, how to lead our lives and whether to love or not. This seemed to be the most important change in me, the choice to love, to break the pattern I'd been repeating in all my relationships with men. I had pushed them away when something didn't go my way, albeit this was usually a build-up, and quite often justified. But I didn't discuss it. I just discarded them, like disposable objects that had a use-by date (a common term I know for relationships). Do we often give the other person a chance to grow with us, or are we so arrogant and independent that it's simply *'sorry bud, my way or the high way!'*

It was not only my reversal of feelings but his also. We all know that a relationship is a series of compromises. Some of us can bend in the wind like willow trees, leaning into the other, whilst others are like rigid oaks, sturdy, steadfast, and deep-rooted. The second year had been different to the first. I had accepted his lack of appreciation at not acknowledging our anniversary, by candidly stating that he was now '*someone to just go out with*'. I know that it hurt him, and somehow my disappointment also cut to my core as I spoke those words, because they became my ongoing truth. He could visit my home where the relationship took place, but he was not really there because I was not accepting him being there. I stopped initiating because I did not want to lead or control, and in doing so, we started to fall apart. We were *not* on the same flight anymore!

In letting go of *expectancy* in relationship, creates a void with a great big question mark - *'where are we going with all this?'*

I didn't want it to go anywhere, and I couldn't sense it going anywhere. I just knew that I wanted more from a relationship. And that is my own interpretation of the word '*relationship*'. Kind of puts another spin on it doesn't it? Because relationship comes with commitment generated through connection. I was losing it; therefore the less time I spent with him, the less I wanted to. Was this just the natural *'use by date'* appearing on our timeline?

Mario and I had the same group of friends, so it was inevitable that we would still see each other from time to time, especially on Social Sundays with the other pub dwellers. I could deal with this until I saw him dance with another woman. He might as well have been making love to her in front of me. '*That should be me*', I thought to myself. '*Well you had your chance, and you let him go, your decision, remember!*' Yes indeed, it was my choice. I had reverted to my old ways, building walls and moats to protect the fort, and I was very good at that because I had done it so many times before. A master builder of soul protection, a blanket thrower… to smoulder the flames of desire! Because I did know that he desired me. I tried to ignore him, but I couldn't.

One evening, at the end of another social Sunday, spent entirely ignoring him, he simply came and stood in front of me and looked straight into my eyes. And I felt him more clearly than ever before. He looked sad, he looked sorry, and he cut right through the ether to my very soul without saying a word. We simply stood there gazing at each other, and then we hugged. It was a mother of all hugs, with neither of us letting go, until he said "well I guess I'd better go home now, I'm going into hospital tomorrow for my hernia operation" (Such a great reminder of our age and mortality, when you have these sorts of passing conversations) and off he walked.

The very next day, after a sleepless night, I called him before he went in for his hernia operation. I needed to tell him what I'd felt the night before, and how that simple act of coming to me and acknowledging '*us*' was just so powerful. What was supposed to be a relatively simple keyhole surgery procedure, turned into a major six-week recovery after the surgeon accidentally nicked a hole in his bladder during the operation. This led to an abscess developing around the newly nicked wound in his abdomen and being hospitalised once more as they tried to heal the internal wound and stabilise his blood sugar levels. Of course, I visited him regularly in hospital, which developed into a realisation that I cared deeply for him. He had somehow managed to turn on my *empathy* switch, and this lead to a quiet and positive discussion about what we could expect from our relationship if we were to move forward again. It was the discussion we should have had six months prior, which showed mutual respect for our feelings. The slow move back to each other was fine, and I was far more accepting of what we were together, united in a relationship rather than being *just friends*. I could accept all that he had to offer me, because I understood the value of one day at a time, and living in the moment. Sometimes you cannot force something, which has its own agenda anyway – *love!* On that subject, I think we tend to homogenise the topic of love, with a romantic expectancy. But it simply is sometimes about *choice*, and this was my decision to choose to *love* rather than expect something more from my partner. I should add here that Mario was not a wealthy man, but he was generous rather than stingy, and he always paid for me when we went out. He was such fun and that's exactly why I chose him in the first place.

We resumed our relationship, but nothing changed. He still expected to stay over and consume my whole weekend, whereas I found myself wanting him to go home so that I could have my days to myself. I was still feeling confused about everything; my expectations, which had crept in to undermine us and his expectations of what a girlfriend is to him, (which I wasn't fulfilling). Nothing changed. Neither of us could make the required compromises for the other.

At the start of our third year, he stated that he wanted to be a larger part of my life, and I realised that I could not give this to him, which led me to write my final farewell - by letter. Before I did this I asked for a sign. I loved signs, and got inundated! It was a given that the signs would be in the form of music, that was our world. During the day, three songs made a highlight performance for me. I accidentally came across a dance video of Mario teaching me to dance, to Tracey Chapman's *'Sorry'*. That's a biggy! At the supermarket *'Stand by me'* (our song) played to remind me of what we were or could be if I stuck it out. In the car, *'Besame Mucho'* (Italian for Kiss me a lot) played on the radio. Mario had complained that I didn't initiate kissing enough - lately.

As I wrote my goodbye, I realised I was making the wrong *choice* that it should always be *love*. No matter who, and despite their faults and demands on us, *choose* to love them. I was discovering *unconditional love* – finally! That choosing *love* changes everything. The goodbye letter was relegated to the bin.

And so there I was; believing I was the creator of my own reality when fate intervened and I was handed another script!

Neither of us believed favourably in commercially celebrated days such as Xmas, Mothers Day, Fathers Day, or Valentines Day for that matter. Anniversaries are different and personal. When Valentines Day rolled around and Mario decided to take me out for dinner, I was actually quite surprised. However it was not to be, and on his way to collecting the rose for me, he got the call from his distraught daughter in law in America, who informed him that his son had committed suicide.

Mario was blindsided, and the ripple effect flowed through to our relationship. Mario's vibration naturally changed; when you lose someone tragically you might think that you have to push through – to get to the other side, but sometimes there is no other side, there is no pushing through, but rather there is absorption, adjustment, acceptance. Grief is not something you complete, but endure. It is not a task to finish and move on with; rather it becomes an element of you. I could sense his sadness and his grief. We were still in sync, however, for death had dealt us both a wild card. Within weeks of this tragic occurrence, I received the sad news that my first husband had a brain tumour, with an eight-week life expectancy prognosis. We both knew that our time had come, grief and sadness had landed, therefore our dancing on the surface came to an end. Life as we knew it in our relationship, and for whatever reason we had come together to experience had resolved its mission. So we let each other go and accepted it this time with grace and dignity, remaining as dear friends ongoing.

Before we can begin a new phase in life, we must sometimes first achieve closure of the current stage we are in, simply because many of life's experiences call for closure. The period of completion, rather than being just an act of finality, is also one of transition. When we seek closure, we derive an understanding of what has happened from an experience. It also helps to release feelings of anger or uncertainty regarding the past, which assist in honouring our life experiences, whether good or bad - allowing us to emotionally lay to rest issues that may be weighing us down. In part, this was one of the reasons why I offered to assist my dying ex-husband. I knew he had never forgiven me for leaving. I needed to go back. I went for him - but I also went for me and hopefully *our* closure.

To conclude part one of my book (about art imitating life) I confess that my painting practise is a deeply personal analysis of the rich tapestry woven by my own hand, a collage of beginnings and endings that run together like still-wet paint. The cathartic process of having an affair with my own heART, by knowing (and loving) myself first, helped me understand that the sum of all my past experiences made me who I am today. After all, shouldn't the most important relationship in your life be the one you have with yourself?

Transcendence is the power to be born anew,
to make a fresh start, to start a new leaf,
to begin with a clean slate, to enter into a state
of grace, and to have a second chance.
Transcendence makes no reference to the past,
whether your past has been overflowing with
victories or filled with defeats.
When you enter a state of transcendence
you are able to create a new life,
unburdened by both the victories
and the defeats of the past.
Transcendence is more than just the realisation
that the past is over.
It is also a realignment of all the dimensions
of yourself with the very source of your life.

- Robert Fritz

PART 2

LIFE IMITATING ART

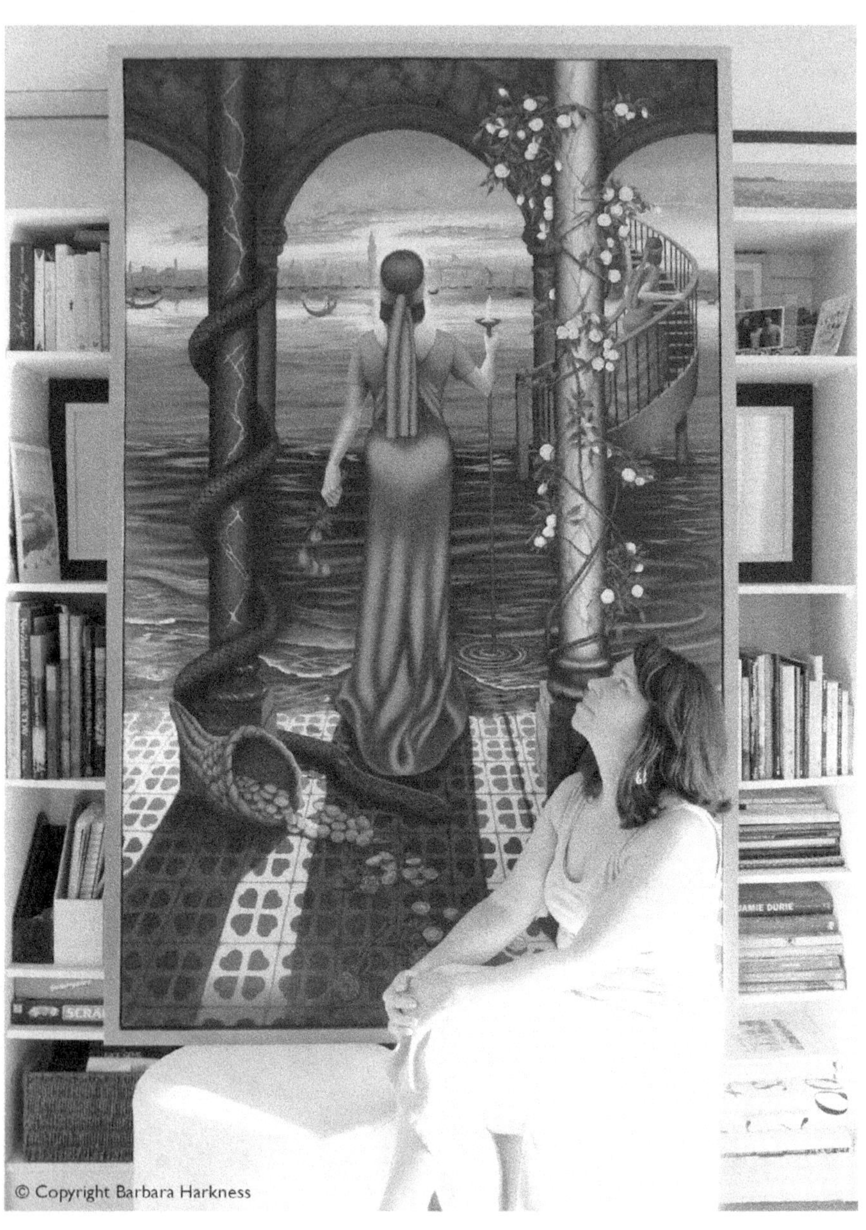

The Magician
mark I

Chapter 9

I had another dream

"The heart has its reasons,
which reason does not know..."
- Blaise Pascal

Slowly I said goodbye to friends, lamenting that I didn't know when I would be back, …because I truly didn't know how long *all this* would take. But I did know this; in my heart of hearts, I knew that I was embarking on a necessary journey, which would continue well after Bob had gone. I trusted my intuition, and the decision to care for someone I had once loved deeply, the man I bore children with, was a decision I made without a second thought. I wanted the consent of our sons, but the final decision, of course, was Bob's. The prospect of spending his final days as a family again filled him with elation, and so I chose once more to be a part of *his life* and *his* departure from Gaia. I gathered our family, to be with him in his final days.

We all know how timing is everything; the painting project had come to an end, my cat Galiano had recently (and conveniently) died, which left no personal obligations, apart from my air B&B, which could be easily managed by simply hiring a cleaner.

A dear friend said to me in response to my decision, "you're standing at the water's edge now aren't you?"

I replied, "yes, I'm ready to go in!"

And my soul spoke to me in a dream that night, which endorsed my decision.

And my soul spoke to me in a dream that night, which endorsed my decision.

I had been left behind somehow and missed my ride to where I was going, on a journey….to somewhere. It wasn't clear in the dream, however, I assume it was to Casuarina, in Northern New South Wales, Bob's home.

There was an urgency to get to my destination somehow...when a large rickety old bus came along and I knew that I had to get on it, even though it looked very unsafe and was extremely old. It was the only ride available! There I was in this large cumbersome vehicle, sitting on my own staring out to my left. Just the driver and I were on board. We were navigating our way around a mountain cliff; you know the sort where it's a one-way passage, and the road is really tight, so a bus is extremely hard to get around those corners. Solid rock on the right, sheer drop to my left, going at a snail's pace to navigate the treacherous situation. But also on the left was the ocean, and the waves were so large that they reached the road halfway up the mountain, and I was on equal viewing with their luminosity. Soft, emerald green flowing waves, the same colour as the sea in my painting, which appeared like giant tidal waves, reaching to the height of the mountain road – in fact they were right at my eye level. Yet I felt no threat. Instead, the waves appeared to be welcoming me with their softness.

The dream felt ethereal and sublime, treacherous but beautiful, and again in full technicolour vision. Was this my looming project with Bob? Did the soft luminous ocean on my left represent spirituality, versus the solidity of the rock wall earthly existence to my right? The left and right aspect was a very strong message (feeling) in the dream. The left side of the body is often regarded as the feminine receiving side and represents the mother. The right side of the body is often regarded as the masculine side and represents the father. I did not know at the time of the dream, that Bob's brain tumour was lodged on the right side of his brain, but in turn, affected the control of the left side of his body. The tumour would lead to eventual complete paralysis. Upon re-reading this dream months down the track, I now understand that the driver of course is my soul, the bus - Bob's body, the encumbrance of the body, as large, and difficult to maneuver, was a sign of the things which lay ahead. And of course, I had 'chosen' to go along for the ride!

Chapter 10

Bob's got a brain tumour

"Choices are the hinges of destiny"
- Anon

Bob chose to refuse chemo treatment, which could have prolonged his life a few more months instead of weeks. He had been through that process before and now accepted his fate, rather than endure the debilitating chemo treatment, which nearly kills you anyway. Upon his refusal of chemo treatment, they shipped him off to a palliative care hospice full of old people waiting to die, even whilst he was quite actively walking and talking and leading a normal life. The place was old and shabby like the poor worn souls who resided there, awaiting their imminent fate. Death's waiting room: *'The Hotel California - You can check in but you can never leave'*, which was his feeling upon waking after his first night there.

So, he called his brother and asked to be collected. He thought he would work it out from there. He felt reasonably normal, however, with his prognosis; it was not practical that he returned to his home, eight hundred kilometres away, with no assisted care. Which of course is when I became involved.

He was naturally distressed about the situation and did not want to be a burden to anyone, which I thought was so unjust, considering the circumstances. You see, how Bob ended up in Sydney, away from his home, was through his desire to help others. His older brother had fallen into a state of depression and was heading for aged care if he didn't get out of hospital and off the drugs, he was on. Bob cared for his oldest brother at home, cooking meals and being good company for him. He put him back on track. Always selfless, with a deep desire to help others seemed to be his thing in life now that he had retired. It was during one of these acts of assistance (moving house for our younger son), that he started bumping into things. His judgment seemed to be impaired; he clipped a car's side mirror travelling too close to the left, and then over judged the curb rather hard whilst parking. He then swiped a car whilst overtaking, and so he pulled over and called an ambulance. Brain scans confirmed the results he did not want to hear but unfortunately expected, nonetheless.

From the age of 54, Bob suffered from debilitating rheumatoid arthritis. He was treated for his condition with a drug called Methotrexate; commonly used for rheumatoid arthritis, auto-immune diseases and cancer (including Leukaemia). It is advised to not combine this drug with alcohol, but Bob liked a drink or two. He never modified his diet to try and treat the cause; rather he relied on drugs to alleviate the symptoms. I call this a band-aid effect because the sore never really heals properly. I believe that a modified diet can treat most ailments and this just makes common sense to me. I think we eat too much, drink too much and I think that our western consumer lifestyle is killing us! I know, that's not a revelation!

Bob never modified his diet to suit his condition, so at the age of 66, he developed MDS (Myelodysplastic Syndrome), which is the pre-cursor to Acute Myeloid Leukaemia. The doctors advised he stop taking Methotrexate immediately. There is a lot of controversy around this drug, which I cannot speculate on because I am not a medical expert, and so I won't. I have researched much on the Internet only to find that it needs to be administered in the correct doses and when overprescribed can lead to fatal consequences.

A complete stem cell transplant from his youngest brother (who was a perfect match) saved his life at the time of his first bout with the disease. This gave him six more years of life.

Four years after the remission, the Leukaemia returned in his spinal and brain fluid, which required a tap inserted into his brain for the chemo to be directly administered. His condition was so dire during this procedure that he ended up with no neutrophils in his blood at all. Neutrophils are a component of white blood cells, which help fight infection, and are commonly killed off through chemotherapy in an effort to fight cancer as well. Chemo kills off most neutrophils, however, once the chemo ceases, the body regenerates. But if the neutrophils are gone completely, death is imminent. His brother started to write Robert's eulogy, and the doctors said, "he is in the hands of God now, we have done all we can. PRAY for a miracle!"

Now, I've heard GOD used candidly as an acronym for **G**eneral **O**verall **D**irector recently and liked it because I think a lot of us find it hard to define God; that omnipresent miracle maker that resides in us all. So, I rephrased it only slightly (my spin on it) to **G**rand **O**verriding **D**esigner; the following dictionary definitions kind of sat better with me. General Overall Director felt a bit, well, *ordinary!* More to the point; I have a belief that we are the designers and creators of our own lives because this is how I have lived mine, with belief and incredible results. Whenever I have lost faith (in myself) life got messy. If you maintain your integrity and truth, then your life opens up in ways that are quite simply - Grand! What do you think? Hey, this is just my spin on G.O.D, as everyone is entitled to his or her own beliefs in this day and age.

Definition of G.O.D

Grand:

- *Magnificent and imposing in appearance, size, or style.*
- *Large, ambitious, or impressive in scope or scale.*
- *A person of high rank and behaving in an appropriately proud or dignified way.*

Over-riding:

- *More important than any other considerations.*
- *Extending or moving over something, especially while remaining in close contact.*

Designer:

- *A person who plans the look or workings of something prior to it being made, by preparing drawings or plans.*

A miracle indeed happened for Bob. The family left him in the ICU that night expecting him to pass away, only to find the next day, that the neutrophils had rejuvenated in his blood. The doctors were stunned because they had never witnessed this before. Once the neutrophils are gone, that's it, they're gone and so is the patient. But he pulled through, with a miracle and grace of G.O.D. The doctors, however, left the tap in his skull for next time - because there was always going to be *the next time*.

The brain tumour was diagnosed some sixteen months after this event. And this time it was inoperable, terminal. Or was it - considering he had fought through and conquered death twice before? I think more to the point was the fact that Bob did not want to go through the trauma of chemotherapy again, and therefore he finally accepted his inevitable fate. He'd had enough. He was 73 years old.

Max (our youngest son) spent two days on a road trip delivering his father to Casuarina, a coastal town in Northern New South Wales, where he had a lovely brand new townhouse. Knowing it would be the last journey they would make together made it very special. Daniel (our eldest son) flew back from Vancouver after the completion of a film project, appropriately timed with his father's illness and imminent departure. Bob was walking, still conversing and happy to finally have both sons with him in his home, and so they downed a few beers on their first night together, followed by a nice bottle of wine over dinner. I don't know whether the alcohol was responsible, or his spirit had been holding it all together until Dan arrived, but that night he went down like a pack of cards. The effect of the brain tumour was starting to take hold and the left side of his body quite suddenly went into paralysis. He needed help in getting to the toilet during the night, every hour, on the hour. He was in his own home, the boys had arrived and I was only a day away...and so he relaxed and let the process begin.

By the time I arrived the next day, I had a very sombre picture painted to me in the car on the way to the house from the airport.

"Mum, I don't think I can do this! Dad's almost a vegetable, he can't walk anymore, I haven't had any sleep, and I've seen far too much of dad's bits! Besides, sometimes the role of the family is to be in a comforting support role, not that of being his actual caregiver."

I didn't reply or offer a comment. *This was not the plan, and surely, he couldn't go downhill that fast?* I'd wait to see for myself before I passed judgment on the situation in the morning.

He rallied a little after I arrived, but was bedridden since the incident. He had no more alcohol, and we limited his liquid intake after 6 pm. He still required assistance to the toilet, but rather than all three of us jump out of bed to his aid, which we did the first night I arrived, took it in nightly turns to be his assistant, whilst two of us got a good night's rest, - sort of. He became semi-independent, with the aid of a four-pronged walking stick, and managed to hobble his way to the toilet for a week, dragging his left leg and bumping into door-frames due to the tumour's effect on his physical spatial judgment. That was until he fell over one night trying to get back into bed, and came down with an almighty crash on the bedroom floor. We realized of course that it could have been into the shower screen, or doorframe and not the soft carpet of the bedroom. After that, it was a matter of both sons carrying him to the toilet, then throwing him up onto the bed afterwards, and dragging his helpless body into a reasonably comfortable position. But it was his bed, and he was happy to be in it. My role was one of cleaning, cooking, making sure Bob was comfortable with clean sheets and blanket weight, which was ever-changing depending on the time of day or night. I knew this was going to be my role and I accepted it with grace. Someone had to do it! I questioned at this stage whether I had done the right thing by asking our sons to be a part of their father's final days, or was this just my own personal journey of atonement I wanted them to witness?

At Max's suggestion, we visited a palliative care facility located in the hinterland behind Tweed Heads, with the view of taking Bob there. It was called a *'retreat'*, run entirely by volunteers and the generous donations of the departing patients. You still had to go on a waitlist, but the average time in this place was only one to two weeks, so availabilities were opening up daily. The Wedgetail Retreat had professional nurses who assisted with the dying process, along with genuine caring volunteers who cooked and cleaned for the patients. It was a house in a rainforest environment with accompanying songbird life. It had a big wide verandah, not a lot of bedrooms, (half a dozen) a common room with a piano and lots of couches, and of course a hospital dog. The relatives would often stay for the duration with the patient in the room, however, this was optional.

The volunteers were so kind, they showed us the house facilities whilst delivering beautiful stories of the people who had passed through their doors and onto the other side. I found myself wondering what sort of person would want to do this job permanently, let alone one that did not pay. I answered that question pretty quickly along with the decision that Bob wasn't coming here, and I wasn't going to let anyone else care for him whilst I was able to. The act of compassion is an addictive one. To give yourself to another with no expectation is such a rewarding gift, and there is no comparison with money because you operate in a different realm.

We returned from Wedgetail Retreat with a boot full of medical supplies to assist our mission; potty wheelchair (which he adamantly refused to sit on), disposable gloves, pee bottle (again refusal) adult diapers (definitely not) adjustable food trays (yes, these were accepted) and the ammunition of determination that we were going to do this thing *at home*.

I knew nothing about how to care for a dying person. I'm not a nurse, but you don't have to be. You just have to be human. Knowing some finer details about him, having been married for 20 years, I decided to take a few things with me for his entertainment, rather than rely on what was already in his home. This consisted of a rainforest CD because I knew he loved the sounds of nature (seriously, we'd had an LP of Australia's native bird calls - it was his favourite to play on a Sunday afternoon!) and the book I chose from my library was *The Alchemist, by Paulo Coelho* – not sure why, but it somehow beckoned to me (Bob's profession had been chemical engineering).

During my search for a luggage padlock, I found my wedding ring and the first gift he ever gave me (a pair of earrings) in a small jewellery box. I tucked this away in my bag for sentimental reasons too.

Everything has a story, doesn't it? These small items relay a tale, precious to only us, but when we share, they become a connection to the reader because of a possible similar experience. Prior to our marrying, I'd only known Bob for around three short months before he departed for job opportunities in America. He was born in the USA (of Australian parents) and had always wanted to go back to discover the land of his birth. That was his plan when he met me and so from day one, I had known that he was going to fly out of my life one day in the not-too-distant future. He had given me the earrings when he departed for America. When he handed me a small box, what I was hoping for was a ring with a proposal of marriage. Perhaps this was the moment we both realized where we were headed anyway. He told me that every time I wore them, they would whisper the words *'I love you,'* in my ears. I wore them every day. He proposed five days later, over the phone - from America.

Three months worth of landline phone calls, five plane fares between the continents, and a wedding later, we were so broke, all we could afford were a couple of rings which cost $10 each. Promises to buy more elaborate ones later, when we were flush with funds, never eventuated, and this never mattered either. It was my wedding ring, and I was going to farewell my husband, this time forever, and so it came with me on this last visit.

The CD never got played - what was I thinking - does anyone still own a CD player? But he did live in a bird paradise, and the birdsong was very active for most of the day. There were even a few butcherbirds Bob would feed with fresh mincemeat. The birds came right into the house demanding to be fed when he was late with their breakfast. These days they would sit on his cane handle whilst he hand-fed them. Simple pleasures.

I started to read the Alchemist to him in small doses during the day and at night; it often sent him off to sleep. It was an apt choice of literature to read, and we would dissect the book's content, from the previous day's reading before moving into it again. He was such a gentle recipient of this activity, because it didn't demand any in-depth conversation from him, and I think he liked hearing my voice. It took his mind away from himself, and through the story, we were connected once more. I had forgotten the storyline, and in re-reading it, discovered that I had chosen the book as much for me, as I had for him.

Paulo Coelho wrote The Alchemist in just two weeks in 1987. Whilst it is not a long story, he explained that he was able to write at this pace because the story was *'already written in his soul'*.

The Alchemist was first released in 1988, and though it sold well, was not until some 20 years later, that it finally took off and became an international bestseller. It has sold more than 65 million copies and been translated into 56 different languages, becoming one of the best-selling books in history and setting the Guinness World Record for the most translated book by a living author.

The book's main theme is about finding one's destiny; discovering what your Personal Legend may be. This is interesting from the perspective that Paul fought his parents' conservative desires for his future because he only wanted to be a writer (perhaps his soul already knew this). An allegorical novel, The Alchemist is about a young Andalusian shepherd called Santiago, who has a recurring dream. The dream speaks to him and tells him he will find treasure at the base of the pyramids in Egypt.

So, he sells his flock of sheep to seek his destiny in Egypt, only to have his savings stolen by thieves. He is in a foreign land and does not know how to speak this language – and so he is forced to learn. He takes a job for a year with a crystal maker and value adds to this merchant's business and is rewarded handsomely. Santiago has learned how resourceful he is in the material world. He joins a caravan to cross the desert to Egypt and befriends an Englishman who is seeking the Alchemist. They bunker down in the middle of the desert to avoid warring tribes, and this is where Santiago meets a beautiful girl named Fatima with whom he falls in love. By this time Santiago has learned so many of life's important lessons. However, his real lessons are more about listening to his heart, and the messages he is receiving from within. He discovers that love, like your Personal Legend, comes directly from the Soul of the World.

While walking in the desert one day, Santiago has a vision of an upcoming battle between the warring tribes. He rushes back to warn the elders of the oasis (where the caravan was temporarily staying). When his warring vision becomes reality, they offer him a position as a counsellor. Santiago considers staying at the oasis with Fatima, but the Alchemist finds Santiago and tells him that he will lead Santiago to his treasure. Fatima also encourages him to continue his journey, for she is a wise young woman and instinctively knows these things; that he must seek his own Personal Legend before he can offer her anything, and so she encourages him to leave.

Almost to the pyramids, Santiago and the Alchemist are taken prisoner by another warring tribe. The Alchemist tells the tribesmen that Santiago is a powerful magician who can turn himself into the wind. The tribesmen are impressed and will spare the lives of the men if Santiago can prove this miraculous act. Slight problem; Santiago has no idea what he is doing! He follows the advice of the Alchemist and after three days of meditating, Santiago uses his instinctive knowledge. First, he asks the desert, then he asks the wind, then he asks the sun, and finally, he asks the Soul of the World. Immediately, the wind whips up into a massive dust storm and then subsides as quickly as it arrived, proving to the tribesmen that he has magical powers. Santiago and the Alchemist are spared and set free by this miraculous act of taming the wind.

The Alchemist takes his leave of Santiago, knowing that he has shown him how to transform himself into whatever he wants to be. Santiago continues to the pyramids, however once there, thieves once more attack him. The thieves ask as to why he is there, Santiago replies that he had a dream of a treasure buried at the base of the pyramids. One of the thieves laughs at him and says that he has had the exact same dream, except that in his dream the treasure was buried in Spain. He goes on to describe in great detail, the place where Santiago used to shelter his flock of sheep. Of course, Santiago goes home, full circle to discover that indeed there is treasure buried in the ruins of his hometown, Andalusia. Now that he is very rich, he can marry Fatima - and lives happily ever after.

The story is simple, elegant and suits all ages. It is a story about us all, continually searching for meaning to our lives, and of course the discoveries as a result, of our true nature. It talks about trusting your heart, and that whatever you do when you really want something to happen, the whole universe will assist so that your wish comes true. And this is the core of the novel's philosophy and a theme that plays throughout.

I found myself reflecting on my own pilgrimage through life, here I was back at my husband's side to complete the journey - to say goodbye. With the benefit of hindsight, one can always look back and see the greater plan, the how's and why's, the reasons and the compromises made. When the story became clear I had asked Bob, "So who do you think Santiago is in our family?"

"Oh, definitely Daniel." He replied.

Daniel travelled a lot for his job, always in a different country, he did not seek to live a conformed life at all, said he gets bored with one place for too long.

"Do you not think it could have been you?" I queried. "When you travelled and lived in London in your twenties, and even when you left me to go to America to seek your fortune there?"

"And you could be Santiago as well, Barbara, perhaps this is the real reason why you left me, to seek your own *Personal Legend*. I understand now that you could not have done this within the confines of the family. You needed to prove your independence and that you could forge a life of your own without me?"

"Yes, you are right Bob, I chose the road less travelled, because I needed to. But we travelled an exceptional road together as well."

I was glad that the book was able to shed a positive light on my reason for leaving the marriage, for I had lived with the guilt, knowing that he had never really gotten over my departure all those years ago.

My return and gathering of our family for Bob's death was an act of personal compassion and a life-altering event for me. It was my choice to leave, and also my choice to return for this final act. It meant a lot to me and I don't think I could have lived with my conscience had I not gone to his side. The universe conspired with all of us. Daniel had just finished a movie project, therefore sought compassionate leave with little disruption to the company. Max ran his own operation with a partner, and as a business owner was probably owed multiple days of leave in lieu of the weekends he often worked. Besides, working remotely these days is always an option. And Bob was getting his dying wish by having his family together once more.

I had wanted *more* from my relationship with Mario, yet here I was back at my first husband's side and am reminded once again of the statement by Morgan Freeman; "If someone prays for patience does God give them patience...or does he give them the opportunity to develop patience? If you pray for courage, does he instantly bestow courage upon you - or provide the situation which requires courage to show up? *If someone prayed for the family to be closer, does he provide an opportunity that facilitates this?"*

Was this love showing up? Was this G.O.D teaching me how to love?

Chapter 11

How to care for a dying person

"No act of kindness no matter how small is ever wasted"
- Aesop

For anyone contemplating the crazy idea of being a caregiver for a person on the way out, there are a few tips I'd like to share. If you didn't think you could do it because it's just too confronting and not your role, then you just might surprise yourself (and others).

The project does not go unrecognized and is acknowledged by community nurses and government-funded facilities that support your efforts, because you are alleviating a small burden from the overloaded hospital system. Once you tell a doctor of your intentions, the network kicks in. They contact you to see how things are running; if you need counselling, a priest, house cleaning, more medical assistance, anything really. They are so kind and will facilitate the right person to help you out with whatever task you need assistance with. We were even issued a *certificate of expected death at home*, which would have negated an autopsy!

I was extremely impressed with the help we received, and feel that if our patient had been more open to the project then we could have seen it through to completion. Ultimately though, Bob was in the driving seat, and we had all simply come along to accompany him for the last leg of his journey. Ultimately, we needed to respect his decisions throughout the process. Maybe I will be a better recipient of death when it is my turn, and my children will certainly know how to do this.

At any stage though, if you feel overwhelmed and can't go the complete distance, then it's OK to opt-out for the conventional palliative care in an institution of your choice. And that was our patient's choice, based on not wanting to burden his family with the ramifications of his paralysis and bodily functions. His dignity was compromised and so he chose to go to hospital for his final days.

A Few Caring Tips:

1: Take care of yourself - you need to be in top form too. Indulge your body at your local Thai massage parlour, and bless yourself for having a healthy one. Go for long walks. We were fortunate to have a glorious stretch of beach 200 metres from the house. Nature is always the answer, so make sure you can get to commune with her on the walks.

2: Tag team with others, so that you get an adequate night's rest every other night. The more caregivers the better, one person is not enough and you need moral support as well.

3: Indulge the patient. A friend of mine, upon learning of what I was about to embark on, gave me an expensive shaving brush and some lovely Italian shaving cream (in a jar, not the foaming stuff). She was a hairdresser. She whispered closely so that no one else would hear, *'A bloke once told me that having someone else give you a close shave with a razor was better than sex. Now I don't know how close you are to your ex, but considering his condition you might want to offer him this service!'* Unfortunately, he refused to let me shave him, preferring the boys to help him with this task, conveniently done over the bathroom basin. To be quite honest with you, I've done a lot of things in my life, but shave a man has not been one of them, so

I was a bit nervous about my inexperienced offer anyway. Once he went to hospital, I noticed that the nurses would shave him every second day. On those days, I poured his shaving balm in my hands and gently rubbed it around his chin and over his top lip - remembering my friend's kind suggestion. These are small things of comfort for the patient - and the caregiver.

4: Read to them; your voice is far more of a comfort than a stranger on a podcast or the news channel. A storybook is also a great way of giving them something to look forward to. Especially when the conversation gets hard. You don't want to be asking them how they are today, because that's just cruel - or their voice has gone.

5: Play music, have a request session. Music seems to be such a direct conduit to the soul and therefore it releases a charge of emotion.

6: Try and be light about the situation. Laughter is a great tonic, so if you can even make a joke about the situation, you will be surprised at how welcome a little private jibe can sometimes be. Of course, everyone is different and this may not suit all types. I would sometimes go into his bedroom in the morning and say, *"you're still here!"* with a sigh, or *"I'm BAAACK!"* And we'd laugh because of our history together.

7: Have a roster of constant company in their room. Don't worry, they sleep a lot too, so it's not totally full-on for the caregivers.

8: Move the living and dining room into their room, provide chairs and small tables so that you can all eat together. Or move their bed into the living room. Sometimes this is more suitable if the house has stairs, or the bedroom is too small.

9: Make sure their bedding is adequate for the temperature. As a body shuts down it is hard to regulate its temperature, therefore the patient will be either too hot or cold. You will need varying degrees of blankets for when they are cold. Cold wet flannels to cool them down when they get too hot.

10: Try and get them to sit in a chair for a few hours a day, rather than being in bed all day.

11: If possible, hire a wheelchair to get out of the house, and go for a run with them. Take them to see the sunrise or sunset, visit their favourite places, or out to their favourite restaurant, or just run around the block on wheels.

12: Make sure the environment is clean and fresh, with new sheets, flowers, a spotless bathroom, scented candles, incense.

13: Say what needs to be said in a positive light and don't bring up unresolved disputes or issues which cause anxiety (for the patient and the caregiver).

14: And lastly, say you love them - often.

One day Dan and I popped out for a walk and came back to find Max with Bob downstairs, sitting on the couch together. He'd had a rally and Max had been able to get him down the stairs into the living room. They had spent the afternoon watching YouTube videos of his favourite artists, George Harrison, Bob Dylan, Paul McCartney. Max had also been serenading him with his guitar. Music is like knitting the fibres of memory, with the sense of hearing, heightened by melody, connected by words of poetry, which resonate deep within us. How often do we hear a song which can bring us to tears, whether by distant memory or simply by the beauty of the sound - this is the true essence of being human so that we can feel emotion. If death could evoke so many deep emotions, then I saw the beauty in it. Their father was leaving, and they had time to say their goodbyes privately and in exactly the way they chose.

This was the last time he came downstairs, the effort just too great to get him back up to his bed. I had set his room up with plastic outdoor chairs and small tables so that visitors could have a chat and we could all eat together. Dinner was now served in his bedroom, where we reminisced old memories and told stories the boys had never heard, about how we were before they were born. Even though Bob and I had been divorced longer than we had been married, the gap in between suddenly dissolved, and *time* became just a word. Time was something he no longer had, and so we all learned to live very much in the present. We also didn't know how *it* was going to happen; therefore, every day was precious. These were his final days and we wanted to make them matter. This was the purpose in bringing my family together so that we could sit and watch George Harrison ruminate on life and the Universe, listen to Barry Gibb and Celine Dion sing *'Immortality'* together, read *The Alchemist* till he dropped off to sleep, play DJ requests from all four of us, sit on his bed, lie with him, sing with him - and cry with him.

He told me they had been two of the best weeks of his life.

And then he said, "I think it's time to go to hospital". Not because *we* couldn't do it anymore, but *he* couldn't, and this was *his* choice. Yes, I will confess it had become very taxing, emotionally and physically. But my rewards in life now were measured by the words *'thank-you'*, which came from his heart - and touched mine.

Chapter 12

Fourteen days in - and now the timer is on

"Start by doing what's necessary, then do what's possible, and suddenly you are doing the impossible"
- Francis of Assisi

"Does someone want to ride in the back with him?" asked the ambulance paramedic.

Both of my sons looked at me and replied, "we think you should, mum".

My sons had just assisted the paramedics to carry their father's limp, helpless body down the stairs in a sling. I'm sure they were also dealing with their own emotions, knowing that this was the final curtain once those ambulance doors closed. I'd called the ambulance because neither of them could do it, and had stated so. Once I was on the phone, I was also overcome with emotion. Giving the patient's details, the reason why we needed assistance and verbalising it made it all too real. This was it, time to say goodbye to our patient. The good times we'd had over the past two weeks were now over. I had wanted to have said goodbye in his bedroom, where *he* was in the comfort of his own bed, where *he* could have just gone to sleep and never woken up - a peaceful departure was what we had all hoped for. No longer able to alight from his bed, made his bodily functions a burden he could not tolerate with his dignity intact. That damned brain tumour, paralyzing his body, had won out. He chose hospital for his final two weeks (which we thought would be only days owing to the tumour's aggressive nature).

During the hospital admittance procedure, the doctor was discussing the details of his condition with him, when Bob indicated he needed to pee.

"Oh, no problem, I'll get a bottle for you to go in."

"No, I don't want to go in a bottle", he replied.

"You're in hospital, mate. That's just how it's done here when you can't get out of bed."

Rather than call a nurse, he just donned some rubber gloves and helped him with the whole procedure. *Of course*, I thought, I should have donned the rubber gloves and held *it* for him, just like the doctor did - made it appear like a normal procedure that is part and parcel of living (and *not* dying). I had so wanted to keep him at home for longer, for all our sakes, if only I could have gone the distance, if only, if only, if only....

The next day when I visited, he said to me "oh, this is not good, is it? I don't like the bed; it's not my bed. The food's not as good as you make, I don't like the view and it gets hot in here."

"Sorry mate, this is as good as it gets. You have to find your own way out of this one." I replied, trying to be candid about it, but the humour was now lost. We had relinquished control to the authorities in an institution, and Bob now got *visitors* who came - and left.

That night I had a dream ...

I was entering a lift; the usual steel doors opened and I walked in with other people. But as they closed I found myself alone, and the lift had become a circular room with a low ceiling, the walls became wooden ..... beautiful, smooth timber. I ran my hands around the circular room looking for the lift buttons to press....up <down>open<> but there were none....help!

Wow, the realisation that I could not contact anyone, or get out, was very frightening indeed. Dreams are such shouters sometimes, not whispers at all. They talk directly to our subconscious, often at a very conscious level. Was this the empathic process awakening in me, by feeling Bob's hopeless situation through the language of dreams?

When Bob entered into his final days and appeared to be sleeping, the nurses told us that hearing was the last sense to go. Upon knowing this, I decided to write him a letter. A few days earlier he had said to me "I'll see you in the next life Barbara, and maybe we will have that little girl you so wanted."

I simply smiled and indulged in his comment. But I felt a deep sense of completion through our soul's contract during this lifetime. Yes, when we met there was an immediate connectedness, which was both familiar and comforting as if we belonged to each other. We had both learned important life lessons from each other, which I felt had completed our karmic debt. For whatever reason, I sensed that my coming back to see him through, was an acknowledgment of this.

I visited him in hospital on my own, because I wanted to read him my letter. He was now unconscious and not responding to visitors. I sat by his bed and read quietly to him, hoping that he would awake and talk to me once more.

April 26th 2019
Dear Bob,

It has been 44 years since I last wrote to you and I will confess it has been confronting to pack up your life during the process of caring for you also. However, it feels strangely comfortable being here.

I have read to you during the past weeks, The Alchemist and we have discussed the characters in the story, particularly Santiago; his adventure in search of treasure, but ultimately how he finds himself right back where he started from. When you left me to go to America, this was something you had to do, and I let you go, of course. It is never anyone's place to hinder or stop another from experiencing their own journey, as it was my will and my choice to leave you, because of my deep desire for independence and self-discovery; this was my only reason for leaving you.

I'm so sorry for hurting you, and our sons. I can only hope that you have finally forgiven me too. This means a lot to me at this time, to be able to say that, "forgive me". Here I am at your side, I did read the fine print, - not necessarily 'till' death do us part, but 'when' death do us part.

There was another path of course - the 'what if I had stayed' one, which confronts me now. Whilst we both know that there have been regrets and remorse in many ways. Like Santiago on his journey, we have come full circle to meet at the end, and recognise the place for what it is. Home.

I am enjoying your home, this place you chose to spend the remainder of your days, albeit for a short time. I find it quite ironic that I am here in many ways, sharing your retirement dream, enjoying the beautiful environment of Casuarina.

I have been swimming in the ocean daily and enjoying the warmth of the sea temperature this far north. The ocean has a strong undercurrent, the waves throw me around, and sometimes knock me right over. I love it though because being immersed in the water reminds me of how life isn't always smooth, or predictable - but sometimes turbulent and surprising.

Sometimes a dangerous little rip takes me out too far, and I have to swim against the current to get back to shore. Life is like that, isn't it?

It has been written in the stars, as it has been in songs, and upon both our hearts, that we should meet again. And I am glad that I found you in this lifetime on Gaia, for the lessons we learned from each other. Thank you, Robert, my husband, and father of my children, for the wonderful life we had together.

With love Barbara

He didn't move or flinch. I simply hoped that he heard my words, kissed him and left.

The following day, when we visited, it was as if his spirit told him we were coming, and he turned his head toward us, opened his eyes and called my name, as the three of us entered his room. We thought he was having a bit of a rally, and we would be able to chat. But that was it, the very last sign of communication we had from him. He became comatose until he passed away a week later.

I felt that he had made a supreme effort to acknowledge my letter, by calling my name - well I hoped so, it meant a lot to me - that one gesture of acknowledgment.

Chapter 13

A case for euthanasia

"The dead cannot cry out for justice.
It is the duty of the living to do so for them."
– Lois McMaster Bujold

From the time Bob entered hospital it took a little over two weeks for the process of dying to complete. I will admit that we could not care for someone who was paralysed and bedridden because he was too proud to have us look after his personal needs.

He confessed to being scared, he became anxious about the unknown, and so yes there was fear, - but why draw it out for two whole weeks? He went from small meals twice a day at home, which I believed was appropriate in assisting a body to shut down, to three-course meals, three times a day! I advised him to stop eating so that he wouldn't have to expel it either. Honestly, I think they make the job so much harder than it needs to be!

Eventually, the brain tumour paralysed his throat muscles, so he lost the ability to swallow food or even suck water through a straw. They started the morphine at this stage, even though he was not in any distress or pain, which is the only kind thing they could do. I'm sure that without this drug the hospital staff's lives would be quite traumatised, least to say the patient also.

The opportunity to take control of his situation was of course illegal, and we also closed that window when he decided to enter hospital. We had a certificate of '*expected death*', which would have negated an autopsy. He was lucid and pain-free at home, so we were not having those sorts of discussions, rather we enjoyed every day we had for what it was – the present, and a gift. However, when all his muscles were paralysed and he could no longer even sip water, it just felt cruel to let him linger in a body, which had let him down. I include this extract of horribilis from my diary only to make aware of the cruelty of not having the choice of a dignified death.

A catheter has been inserted into his penis, an umbilical cord in reverse, draining what little liquid his body still has. It is the colour of tea. His body is hot owing to the process of shutting down and not being able to control its temperature, even though there is a fan constantly blowing onto him. He cannot move his body at all, and the ability to talk, swallow, or respond in any way to our concern for his pain has also been lost. He cannot open his eyes, nor respond to our questions of concern by squeezing our hand, as he used to. The main indication that there is now pain is his guttural groans and grimaces alongside the only function he has, the movement of his right arm, which goes to his head, his throat and his heart, indicating that there is pain in these parts. Occasionally he will cough and splutter in an effort to clear the phlegm, which is building up in his lungs. His breathing, which has been around seven breaths per minute, is now a steady rasp as he struggles for air. His heart beats quicker than normal, to sustain the depleting life force, and I can see it vibrating his head in a counter-intuitive way to where the damned tumour lies hidden, slowly strangling him from within, and sucking the life out of him. He is reluctantly driving a car - his foot flat to the floor, with the hand brake on, and some bastard has put sugar in the tank, which is leaking throughout the parts, and disrupting the mechanics….

It took five days of this condition before he finally passed away. I even overheard one of the nurses at the station say "Oh my gosh, Mr

Harkness is still here, I thought he would have gone days ago!"

When we got the call at midnight to say we'd better come in because they didn't think it would be long now, we didn't make it there in time. We would have liked to have been there, holding his hand, hugging him, talking to him. Instead, we walked into a room and saw a body, and all we felt was relief that his suffering was now over. We very diplomatically discussed the next procedure in the process of death, collected his belongings and exited the hospital. Not a tear amongst us.

The hospital staff commented that he was so peaceful in his final days and appeared to be in no pain. Well, that was thanks to the morphine, and I was not going to debate death with them. They do a fantastic job in light of how traumatic it must be daily, dealing with so many of these cases. But who knows what he felt throughout those five long days of trying to depart the planet? Uncertainty, fear, anxiety, pain, he was a hostage in his own body with the ravages of cancer eating him alive, tripping out on morphine to aid the long journey. Five days to shut down is a long time!

Through the limited choice on offer, I felt like we had been denied this milestone event of dignified intimacy as a family. Perhaps we already did this when we were at home with him, and this was when his life really ended?

One in four of us will die of cancer, and we all know someone who has. I know this story I am sharing is not unique, but I do believe that it is through the sharing of stories, which connect and help us to make better decisions and choices throughout our own lives.

I have researched the ideas behind *'end-of-life'* assisted suicide, religious and spiritual beliefs on the subject of voluntary euthanasia. These are varied and many, so I won't preach my findings on the subject. This is simply my story, which evolved through the process of observation, and as a result, formed my opinion. We should all have a *choice*, rather than be governed by legislation. This results in the difference between a good or bad death. We were going for the good death, which I felt got taken out of our hands once inside the establishment of palliative care.

I reflect on my friend Billie's recent passing (from cancer). Billie had a remarkable spirit and fought her disease till the very end. She was diagnosed with stage four-bowel cancer with a prognosis of roughly five years. She was the same age as me, so I *know* she went too soon! She had so many operations to cut the cancer out, I lost count. The last one was a tumour behind her eye. She showed me pictures of her eye after the operation. They had neatly cut along her eyebrow, peeled back her entire eye and shaved the tumour off. A couple of weeks later you would never have known what she had gone through. She looked perfect! But the photo of her massive bruised and tightly closed eye, made her look like she had been in a street fight. In many ways, she had and lived to see another day, another week, in this case, it was only months. She'd already had two -hirds of her lungs removed, and half her bowel. She did all of this at the insistence of her two daughters encouragement to fight to live. So, when it came time to accept her fate, they were adamant that she was not going to die in hospital. They rented a larger pad where they could all be together, and when the hard stuff arrived, they did it all. They nursed and cared for their mother; they administered the morphine and cleaned her body. They were my inspiration when it came to my decision to care for Bob, who had also spent far too much time in hospital at death's door, defying all the odds as well.

I know that Bob chose hospital over a home death to spare me the ugly details of caring for his body. I never insisted because he was a proud man, and if choice was the last thing he had, then I was not going to deny him that.

I can only hope that euthanasia is an option when it is my time. Because if not, then I am making my own rules - I always have!

Chapter 14

The home-style memorial…it's easy!

Life is a song – sing it
Life is a game – play it
Life is a challenge – meet it
Life is a dream – realise it
Life is a sacrifice – offer it
Life is love – enjoy it

- Sai Baba

Being a very modest man, Bob didn't want a funeral. He specifically didn't want anyone giving a eulogy, some stranger saying something nice about him at a pulpit, or people drinking to his memory all day. We all collaborated before he went into hospital, and agreed on exactly how his farewell was going to look. Many people like to plan their own funerals, right down to the music (we played his beloved George Harrison - I hope that he gets to befriend old George where he is now). He loved what we finally came up with, and oddly, it wasn't morbid to discuss either, just a rather matter of fact discussion.

When he died, he was simply taken from the morgue, cremated and then collected. This ceremony was a little ritual in itself, requiring identification of my relationship to Bob, - who was now in a box, complete with a cremation certificate, of course, to confirm that he was now *ashes!* The process from death to the collection of ashes takes about a week, long enough to organise a simple memorial. The cremators also organise the paperwork, which is required for a death certificate to be issued. This is separate from the cremation certificate also. I was surprised at how much paperwork is involved with dying, right down to a final tax return! Thankfully death taxes were abolished years ago. I always thought that was such a final insult, wringing the last dollar out of you.

On the day of the memorial, Daniel came downstairs and asked me where his Dad's clothes were. He had played dress-ups in Bob's clothes for fun one day to amuse us – (Bob and I), by being Bob 1970's style, right down to the long, curly, unruly hair! I'd photographed them together, then compared the photos to ones of Bob in the 70s. These are the memories of course that I shall hold forever dear and close to my heart and hope our sons will also. Being as industrious as I am, the clothes had already been given away to charity. However. I had kept one item; his most loved and worn shirt, which was close to 50 years old because I knew he'd purchased it during his time in London when he was in his 20's. It was a very unique artisan shirt, full of embroidered and screen-printed travel motifs. I had found it in a rather mouldy state, but a quick soak in Napisan brought it back to new, no frayed collar, embroidery all still perfectly intact, the screen print Eiffel Tower, Arc de Triomphe and Notre Dame still as vivid as the days when he wore it…everywhere. Notre Dame had burned that very week too. I reluctantly handed over my chosen outfit for the memorial event, for Daniel to wear. He wore it well, and it looked better on him than me. But more so, I know that he wanted something memorable to take with him back to Canada, being as he could not take any of his larger material possessions. Bob had left a photo of us in my bedroom, taken at some fancy black-tie event. I didn't notice the shirt in the photo until I found the actual one and had revived it. He wore it often, from black tie events to casual BBQs. Some things are just so priceless; I would have to make do with the photo because the shirt now belonged to Daniel. I put a love spell on it and gave it over.

Bob's two brothers and their respective entourage had travelled up to Casuarina for the final farewell ceremony. One brother already lived close by. We all met at beach entry number six, which was the path he took for his daily walks. All three brothers along with their wives, three nephews and their wives, one niece and her husband, and five little ones were present. It was an intimate gathering, which was what we finally decided upon. Rather than extend to neighbours in the housing estate, I did let them know of the time we were undertaking this task, in the event they wanted to say their farewells to him as well. As an ode to Bob's Scottish heritage, we organised a bagpiper to play whilst we scattered the ashes into the crystal clear and warm waters at Casuarina. He really loved the idea of a bagpiper; in fact he smiled broadly when we told him what we had planned.

Might I add that it is totally illegal to scatter someone's remains in this manner, but I heartily encourage it, because breaking these sorts of rules makes you feel quite confident and just a little bit rebellious! Ashes are not actually ash, they are gritty and sand-like and besides, no one is going to come and break up your party either. I'm not sure what the fines are - send me the bill if you get one - and I'll tear it up for you!

For the children, I organised a basket of rose petals so that they could have a little scattering amongst themselves at the lower level. I'm not so sure they knew what was going on anyway, and the rose petals create such a lovely added effect, and their evidence lasted for days. The beach was strewn with pretty rose petals well after the event.

I'm sure Bob had a hand in organising the weather on the day of his memorial. There was no wind to speak of - it was *dead* calm! This was a blessing because the usual surf could easily knock you down even in the shallow waters at the shoreline. Not a cloud in the sky, just the clear southern hemisphere renown for its intense shades of every blue there ever was.

As the bagpiper slowly wandered off and disappeared into the dunes, his melodic ancient whine fading into the ether, we slowly made our way back to Bob's home where I had prepared a morning tea for everyone. Rather than speeches, I asked everyone if they would all like to say something specific about a memory of Bob that they held dear. Everyone knew his history, so his life did not need to be repeated to those close. We called these *'the conversations'*. A show-reel of his life in photographs played out on the television, including some intimate moments from his hospitalisation. We decided to share these because he did not want visitors once he went to hospital. The pictures told the story we all knew well enough.

We had only photos of Bob in the small picture frames scattered around the living room, with his brothers, and his sons. Thank you flowers from my sons for my efforts in organising the event sat on the side table. But you can decorate the home in a way that you feel best honours the deceased person's life. In fact, you can do whatever you want, when you design a personal memorial day for a loved one - there are no rules.

Being as many of the family flew up from Sydney, we planned a whole day of family events to remember the day by. To work off our morning tea, we walked four kilometres along the beach to Halycon House at Cabarita, which is probably the fanciest bar in town. We invited neighbours to join us for this, and once there shouted everyone a drink or two. This was followed by a casual dinner at a local cafe with family, and supper back at his house. Finishing up at around 10 pm, I was in awe of this family and how the conversation just flowed and flowed, it never seemed to dry up. Even saying goodbye at the door, another story would pop up, and half an hour later the last guest would finally step over the doorstep and leave!

All up, a simple home-organised memorial day to honour and

celebrate your loved one will cost around $2000, depending on your tastes. It is my opinion that death has become a moneymaking industry, and part of living in the age of convenience. Get someone else to do it, and pay them. There is something far more personal when the affair is *home-grown*, and of course, this takes time to organize. I have been to a few funerals now and have to say that the ones held in halls and homes, and not funeral parlours were by far the most memorable.

In finishing this chapter, I will do so by saying that our sons were stellar in playing their parts during this time. They needed me as much as I need them. We leant on each constantly and in doing so neither of us fell. The process of being with and caring for each other helped to facilitate a *good death* for their father. Children are such gifts, and I cannot imagine my life without them being here. This makes me feel so grateful. At the memorial, I saw the good upbringing, the manners, the responsibility, the hard yards we put in, returned one thousand times over. They were diligent, attentive, supportive, and emotional. They loved the day, just as they'd turned up in action for his last month. They made me realise my role as a mother as well, that this responsibility never diminishes, and that in a way I had come full circle back into their lives as well. We became a tight-knit circle of three. Being together as the original family unit for bob's death was an incredibly bonding experience, and I have never felt closer to my sons. For that I was grateful.

Chapter 15

Reflections on then….

"Love isn't something you find.
Love is something that finds you"
- Loretta Young

We've all heard about the remarkable connection between couples that seem to know within days of meeting, that they would marry. It is usually at the make-or-break three-month mark that the man proposes and life begins as a united front and two become one. That's exactly how we felt once we were married, this happy ever after prospect of building a home and creating a family was all we aspired to and all we dreamed of, the whole scenario of endless possibilities. Innocent, naive, and beautiful, that's what love does to you when you are young. Incredible isn't it, that love could produce so much optimism about determining the rest of your life.

I was only 17 years old and Bob was 29 when we met. I was on a working holiday in Sydney, Australia. It was the typical boy meets girl in a bar sketch *(The Johnnie Walk Wine Bar* - still there today I might add). We spent the weekend together, visiting the tourist sites of that magnificent city I was planning on making my home for a year or so. However, he lived at the top end of Australia in Townsville some 2,000 kilometres away, working as an operational engineer for Queensland Nickel and was in Sydney for a family visit, when I met him on that fated weekend. Australia was such a big country compared to the islands of New Zealand where I was from. We said good-bye after our fleeting weekend encounter, exchanging address details only, on the promise that we would write, then quickly became pleasant distant memories to each other as we got on with our individual lives. But I didn't forget the handsome man I had met that weekend.

I was always wanting adventure and seeking it out at every turn. As fate would have it, six months later we both wrote letters to each other at precisely the same time. I received a letter from him stating that he was coming back to Sydney, before heading off to explore work possibilities in the USA. I'd written to ask if I could come to visit and explore Townsville and surrounding districts (with him). Our letters must have passed in mid-air, so our lives were definitely in synchronistic harmony. A plan was hatched between us, which suited both our travel plans. Our destinies had started to collaborate! I would fly to Townsville and we'd explore the East Coast of Australia together by road, driving 2,000 kilometres back to Sydney town, where he would then depart for the USA. And that is how we fell in love, exploring the magnificent coastline of Australia in his 1964 Kombi van. The vehicle was rusty and dilapidated - it even had those classic wind-out front windows, which was a great way to ventilate the smoke from our cigarettes as we spun out our life stories to each other on the long road trip we were riding toward each other (albeit my stories were considerably shorter than his).

At Rockhampton (the halfway point in our journey) the Kombi clapped out. We probably should have abandoned the dear old thing and flown the rest of the way, but we were having the time of our lives falling in love. It was as if the Kombi knew this and prolonged the journey for us deliberately.

Once we got to Sydney of course, Bob did not want to leave me. The game plan had changed and we spent every single day together, further exploring life with my friends, and his friends, for another whole month.

Until one day he said to me "I have to go, I need to stick to my plan of going to America because I'm running out of money."

"Of course you need to go," I responded, knowing that we couldn't keep playing forever. I needed to get a job as well! Five days after his departure, he called me from that far away land and asked me to marry him.

Our courtship was so very brief, in fact from the time we started the journey in the Kombi van in Townsville, through to the time we finally married in New Zealand, was a mere three months – yet it felt like a lifetime. I wasn't expecting a marriage proposal after such a short courtship! But I said yes, and can confess to being terribly excited at the prospect of being married, even at the tender age of 18. I didn't think twice about it because we were so very much in love and simply couldn't bear to be apart. I was too young to analyse the future ramifications of our age difference, and besides, love conquers all right!

When Bob left for the United States of America, I gave him a book by Max Ehrlich titled *The Reincarnation of Peter Proud.* At 18, I was simply curious about such ideas. I had enjoyed the book and wanted to know if Bob shared similar values. The answer was given to me by way of the following synchronistic sign.

I flew back home to New Zealand for my brother's pending wedding and began planning one for us as well. Bob flew back from the USA to my hometown of Wellington, where I was eagerly waiting for him after our agonising six weeks apart. I'd never experienced anything like this before - he seriously was my first love. Wellington airport was fairly primitive back then, more like a converted hangar with a viewing platform atop the main building, where you climbed stairs to a rooftop to wave goodbye, or await the arrival of your loved ones. I can remember this like it was yesterday, being on that top deck, my skirt billowing behind me (a difficult task considering Wellington winds normally have your skirt up around your ears), holding on to the rails like I was at the helm of a ship, hoping that he would be on the right side of the plane to see me.

When he arrived, one of the first things he blurted out was, "They played it on the plane, and I've been crying in anticipation of seeing you again".

"Played what?" I asked.

"The movie, The Reincarnation of Peter Proud!"

He'd come back to me! I was the envy of my sisters, being swept off my feet and getting hitched in such a whirlwind way, then flying off to America with such a handsome catch I might add. Of course, my mother and father were just relieved that they had relinquished control of their adventurous daughter and that she was now safely being cared for. I was the responsibility of someone else, my new husband.

The wedding was not costly, a typical New Zealand home affair, held in the living room of my parents' house, after a simple Baptist church ceremony. My younger sister had performed bridesmaid duties at my brother's wedding just weeks prior, so I enlisted her along with her ready-made outfit to perform the task again. Dad's Chrysler Valiant was commissioned as the bridal car complete with ribbons and bridal doll (driven by Dad as well) transporting me 1.5 kilometres to the local Baptist church, where a simple wedding ceremony transformed me into a mature married woman. Oh, I can remember being so excited about that, complete with a new name, it was pure reinvention on a visceral changing stage. I was so ready for this new life as a married woman, even though I was only 18. I loved every minute because of being so in love with my husband. I chose a really simple ring (which cost only $10) based on the fact my new husband had gone to such extraordinary lengths to fly back from the USA to marry me in my hometown. We were going to start our new life in debt, owing to all the airfares between continents to pull off this simple but life-changing event. I did not want to contribute anything further to that with expensive jewellery, which did not add any value to our happiness.

Bob was born in Pasadena California, to Australian parents, so this was a pilgrimage for him in many ways. Having US citizenship meant he was always going to take advantage of it at some stage in his life. That opportunity had arrived, and I was now a part of it too. He secured a job at an engineering firm called C.F.Braun. This firm was so ultra-conservative - every single engineer had their own oak-panelled office with a nice oak desk, smack bang in the middle of the room, a swish leather chair completed the austere picture. There was also a dress code, the engineers were expected to wear a suit and tie. Bob did not fit this mould at all, and rocked up on day one in the only suit he had - a tan corduroy number complete with bell-bottom pants, and of course the only sort of tie a guy like this would have in the 70's - paisley! Not only did he buck the Braun dress code (sure he could have started a trend there), but wowed them completely with his mode of transport – a bicycle! When he went to collect it after his first day at work, a parking fine was slapped on it because he had chained it to a tree!

The trees were another story altogether, quite often he would rock up to work on Monday morning to find that they had relocated a huge palm tree over the weekend, or replaced them with oak trees of the same size. This was an engineering feat in itself, and certainly a case of *too much money.*

We, on the other hand, were flat broke. After three months of playing and not working, airfares to the USA, and back again for him, we had taken on a loan to facilitate the start of our married life. But the firm demanded that he buy a decent suit AND a car! Declaring our predicament, I think the company very generously gave him an advance on his salary. Note; these were the days before credit cards!

We purchased a 1964 white Mustang with red leather bucket seats, which was an absolute monster to drive because power steering has not been used on that model! It suited us perfectly, more so than the dark suit Bob had to wear every day. But we all wear suits of some sort don't we, to accommodate what is requested of us?

Our mission in California was to save money to buy a house in Australia and have some fun along the way exploring America. The fact the job was not a good fit for him didn't matter. I could not get a job in my career even though I had been working for three years as a commercial artist, because at 18 in America you were still supposed to be in college. The legal drinking age is 21 in California meant I quite often could not enter a bar, even though I was a married woman and accompanied by my responsible husband 12 years my senior.

The mission to save money for a deposit on a house meant we had to be creative, whilst still exploring this vast state we were fortunate enough to be in. Defiant that the company would not change us - we bought a tent! We'd often escape from smoggy Los Angeles and head out onto the Ventura Freeway to the clean air of the California coast, exploring the towns both south and north of Los Angeles; San Diego, San Luis Obispo, Santa Barbara, Las Vegas in Nevada, even Mexico.

Anything that was within driving distance was a reason for a weekend escape on the road in our Mustang beast. We loved the drive to San Francisco and did this a couple of times on longer trips. Being all loved up in our little red pup tent, camping along the way until we got to San Francisco where we would splash out on a hotel for a couple of nights in the city - this was like replicating the blueprint for how we fell in love. We would then shoot over to Yosemite national park to camp with the bears, and plough on down through the Mohave Desert in one quick run back to L.A, winding the beast up to 100 miles per hour on the super straight desert road - singing loudly at the top of our voices *'those were the days my friend, we thought they'd never end...'* God, I loved the 70's!

I found a song, written and sung by Celine Dion, titled "I remember LA". I was amazed at how accurately the words reflected our past. It was as if she stole a glimpse into our private lives and wrote about it. I love the way songs can relate to your own story.

I remember LA ... seems a lifetime ago ... we were Stars on Sunset Boulevard... what a movie we made. There were days in the sun that have stayed forever young. There were moments in my lifetime that my heart still replays ... there were minutes, there were hours, there were days ... there are moments I still love you the same way ... when I remember LA ... I remember goodbye ... I watched your plane fly out of sight .... love was over, time to close the book ... yet I go back for one last look. How apt these lines in the song were and still are right now, as I reflected on my life with Bob...Going back for one last look. The song never failed to move me.

So, what went wrong you might ask? Absolutely nothing! In hindsight, and knowing how life works, *I joined the dots,* so to speak. When Bob and I married he was 30 years old, smack bang right on his

Saturn Return. A time when he was ripe for a big change in his life and that was marriage, accompanied by the belief that we would be together for the rest of his life. A big decision in anyone's life!

A little about Saturn's Return for the uninitiated; a Saturn Return is an astrological transit that occurs when the planet Saturn returns to the same place in the solar system that it occupied at the moment of a person's birth. This is approximately 30 years, the time it has taken for Saturn to make one orbit of the Sun. The effects of this astrological event are often felt two to three years prior. This transit also coincides with the end of innocence, a time to leave youth behind and get on with the serious stuff of life, like career, marriage, and for some divorce. Basically, it's an assessment of where you are at in life; an analysis of whether you are on track or not. Saturn is often called the planet of Karma, and the taskmaster of the zodiac. During the Saturn Return, whilst there is developmental pressure to achieve more in life, it is highly probable for people to let go of things that no longer serve them; even if this means stepping into the unknown to let life just unfold. Similarly at the second Saturn Return, at around age 56-60, the latter is more often implemented. It's a bit like a life review when you get to ask the hard questions of yourself. The Second Return is also a reminder of our mortality, by questioning whether we are spending our time showing up as our authentic selves.

If we are lucky enough to experience a third Saturn Return (at age 90), there is even more of a desire to let go of things that no longer serve us – especially any ego attachments. At the third juncture naturally, we ask the question *'am I making the most of the time I have left'?*

When I hit 30. I can only describe that feeling as my soul knocking on the door at three in the morning saying *"you have to leave, you have to leave, there is a whole other life out there for you"*. I kept talking myself back into the role of wife and mother because by this time I had everything a woman could want; a beautiful five-bedroom house with a pool, an adoring husband, two sons I loved and whom I knew would come off the worst when I left. I tried to resist but eventually consulted a therapist to find out what was wrong with me. It was the therapist - a total stranger who did not know me (or Bob), that finally shed light on my situation, which I simply could not work out on my own. I can still remember spilling my guts to him through a bucket of tears - an absolute mess! Perhaps he saw the angst I would have endured had I stayed and issued this advice, *"Sometimes we 'help' people to leave - rather than stay"*. The longer I stayed, the more detached and resentful I became. I know now this was my soul resisting, knowing that there was a different life for me with other challenges. It took me six more years to finally convince myself to leave the marriage at age 36. And Bob did not speak to me for ten years afterwards.

Chapter 16

Terms of Atonement

'Without sadness, there is no happiness,
without ugliness, there is no beauty,
without death, there is no life!
To understand the finality of our human existence,
and that time is so limited,
is to appreciate how to live fully in the present.'
- Barbara Harkness

As I packed up his life and sold down the possessions, I was inadvertently also unpacking our history together. Interestingly in art terms to *'unpack'* means to analyse something, to take apart an idea and examine each piece in detail. Unpacking involves a sort of deconstruction, the letters and photos of course being the most poignant examples. Living the final part of his journey was also addressing my conscience for leaving the marriage. He had never forgiven me, and now his pain became mine. I also sensed his loneliness, which became quite palpable during the last few weeks I was there. I felt a deep sense of regret on my part, just as he had for the later part of his life.

Gandhi said, *"life is about the journey, not the destination."* Yet here we were having reached the destination together, having taken separate journeys for much of that time. Now it all felt so fleeting, so short, and so questionable.

I also knew this was what I had been searching for, that part of myself which had not forgiven the act of leaving – even though my journey had been wonderful, there was still the aspect of having hurt someone in the process of taking control of my destiny. That *other side* had never really been addressed and it was time to balance the personal ledger.

I went way back down memory lane to the start of our marriage, through our initial love letters from the time he left to go to the USA, and I'd returned to New Zealand. But I found that most of these letters were to us as a family. Written from an overseas assignment in Jakarta he took in 1988, they touched me deeply. I was reminded of what a good father he was. He was not a risk-taker like me, he was a rock with a good profession, which he endured and stuck to his whole life because he wanted to be a good provider. His engineering profession took us all over Australia, and we were well looked after by the companies he worked for. The Indonesian stint was a three-month trial period, in consideration of a longer-term assignment, to see if it was suitable for the children to be educated there. We'd decided against it owing to the considerable cultural differences. His letters written to us at that time indicated such a beautiful love and concern he had for us. We were everything to him, and reading them now was the right time to reflect on such matters. I found myself looking at the photo I had placed by my bed, of us looking radiantly happy - I was simply glowing and he was wearing the Eiffel tower shirt with a red bow tie. I found myself talking to him - my Bobbi. After all, it was now just he and I in this house, alone at last!

Selling the house was by far the easiest task; it seemed the Universe really had my back during this time. That good old magnetic energy brought the right people to our doorstep, literally! A family who had moved into the townhouse complex via a rented property was in the market to purchase. They were a family of four (plus a large husky dog) who had decided to downsize from their large home, to enable more time together, knowing that their time as a family unit was limited and therefore very precious. When they heard of Bob's condition and that the house might be coming onto the market, they wasted no time in making it known that they were interested. I waited until he had passed before inviting them in for a viewing. I think their decision took all of five minutes and made an offer the very next day. A week of negotiating eventuated in an outcome everyone was happy with. I was interested in this family with teenage daughters and a large dog, who had decided to downsize early. I would have thought that they would be upsizing if anything. But their motive was one I could relate to, owing to my considerable recent downsizing. They wanted to be mortgage-free, so that they could travel extensively with the girls for months at a time, to give them the best education they could; seeing the world.

They went on extended trips overseas and lived in other people's homes for months at a time on a home swap/minding basis, getting to know the countries they visited at a community level. This was their idea of a broad and varied education. Majken was Scandinavian and therefore relished the opportunity to show the girls her homeland.

They were a single income family. Paul worked, and Majken home-schooled their two daughters so that they could indulge their extra-curricular passions for surfing and horse riding when it suited them. The waves are sometimes the best at 9 am, right? Paul had bragging rights to surfing at Black Rocks with Kelly Slater and Thor!

"It doesn't get much better than this Barbara", he told me, one day after they had experienced sharing the waves with one of the world's greatest surfers. I could sense his satisfaction at achieving their family ideology, as he told his story with the utmost joy of how Charlize (the eldest daughter) and Kelly Slater took turns at the waves, who had graciously guided her with some surfing tips as well. Then recognising Thor (Chris Hemsworth) out on the back waves had really made their day!

"Aren't you supposed to be in Rio at a tournament?" Paul had asked of Kelly.

"Naa, it's much better here", he'd replied.

He was right, and I was so happy that they were the family who had chosen to buy Bob's home. It was their intent, to purchase in this particular housing complex, but wanted a property on our side of the street, which had more security and a west-facing aspect; this meant the house got filled with the late afternoon sun. Their intent became our easy passage, and the Universe conspired to bring us together - and it did for so many more reasons, which were highly personal. You see, Bob and I had both wanted to move to this region back when our children were small. My motive was just the same as this familys' was - I wanted a better life for my kids, a free life. However, I had imagined a large block of land where we grew our own food and had lots of pets. The principle is the same. Unfortunately, Bob's sense of responsibility to provide for his family financially had overridden my desire for a more holistic lifestyle, and therefore we continued to follow the corporate path of company jobs which took us all over around Australia. I have to say that this is where we fell down and was when I realised that I did not have a voice in the marriage. I had my role, and it was one of convention, I was a housewife and mother, and Bob was the provider. Don't get me wrong, he was a very good one and I was thankful for his ability to provide very well. I knew that I had the courage and determination to carve out a better life, to throw caution to the wind when it came to living an authentic life. But it was not to be, and we stayed with the company plan, but a little bit of *us* went missing with that decision. I know now that taking the step in life is primary. The destination is secondary. The destination got put on the back burner for another day, perhaps retirement, and only Bob's.

It was ironic that a family with the principles they practised, bought the house because they reminded me of our lost opportunity. It was befitting that this lovely family should be the new owners, and they were a great fit.

A strong sense of karma pervaded my senses after his parting for other reasons also. I had left him, and now he had left me - forever. I'd been able to defend my right to leave, which in his eyes, previously, was wrong. He had finally been able to see that I was a good person and that I did not ruin his life, even though he had held me accountable for not going the distance. Rather, it was his reluctance to live in the present moment and enjoy what life offered him, that created such regret around the end of our marriage contract. I had gone on to live a life full of enriching experiences. I built a business, remarried, travelled the world, divorced again, re-schooled, and became an artist. Bob stayed stuck in the past. He stayed in the same profession all his life, for safety reasons, retired, got sick and died, all the while reverberating his life's regrets, and I was one of them.

It is so important to let go of the past. Whether we make mistakes or not, it does account for who we become or do not become. There is no right or wrong. There is just the fact that you cannot undo what has been done. But you can change perspectives on your views. The experience of our past teaches us how to become better people, who can make clearer judgments for a better future. Nor do our mistakes define us as failures, because every new day we are given is an opportunity to *get it right*, and that quite simply means being consciously present and not somewhere else - certainly not in the past.

Most days during my stay in Casuarina I would go down to the beach to watch the sunrise. This was just one of those simple reminders that every day is a different day.

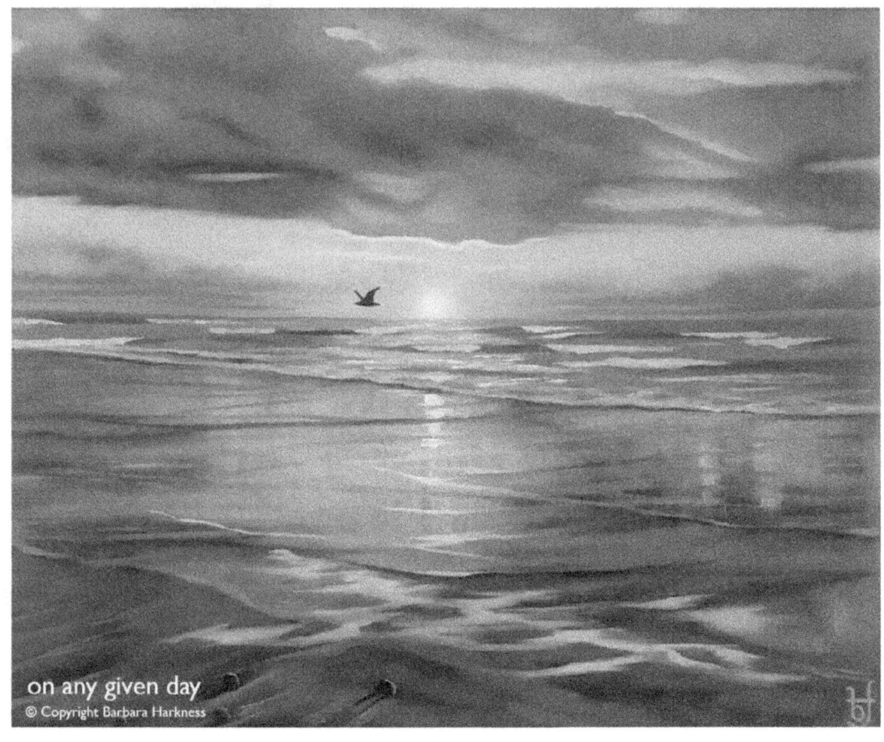

On my first beach sunrise encounter, the whole canvas was covered in shades of grey, small long dense clouds from the base of the horizon, expanding to cumulous fluffy large ones directly above me. Art had made me a witness to the world around me, viewing it as a painting, with details, along with the question, *'how would I make that colour or mark'*? G.O.D does it so well - slowly, and without effort, the edges of the dark greys slowly turned to tinges of pink, a soft baby pastel pink. The colour is more intense just before the main act arrives. The hues intensify in colour to orange, then spread like ink on blotting paper, right before your eyes, until the Grand Over-riding Designer finally appears on stage in a burst of blinding light to introduce the brand new day. A day like no other. I found myself in a natural pattern of gratefulness, just by doing this daily task. Getting up to greet the day, and say *'how lucky am*

I to witness this, how lucky are we, to be alive, to be human.' On my last day in Casuarina, I rose early to watch the sunrise. I felt a great desire to take in as much as I could of this beautiful place during my final week. Sure enough, the sunrise did not disappoint. It was spectacular - the sky was already pink by the time I arrived. I stood at the shoreline watching the sun appear and noticed that the tide appeared to be on its way in. It came to greet me, lapping at my feet with a welcoming lick. *'Hello Barbara'*, the tide said, *'I am going to miss you'*. I felt that the tide was telling me something, and I listened to the whisper, *'it's your turn now, the tide has turned your way'*. At that moment I was reminded of my Magician painting. I had projected my vision into the Universe via the canvas, and here I was, here I had been, and therefore I was. The intent of my painting had been one of searching for myself, for a deeper meaning to my life. I had found it in nature, solitude, through writing, forgiveness, compassion and love of family.

However, I had started to pine for my little home in South Australia some 2,000 kilometres away. I could have stayed on enjoying the Indian summer at Casuarina, swimming in the ocean most days, beach walking and writing this journal, until settlement of the house went through, which was another month away. But the loneliness had started to close in. I had been away for three months; my job was well and truly done. It was time to call in the charities to take the remaining gear away. The unpacking of Bob's life was a true closure for me. I had gone back to say goodbye and to help him, but it was so much more. I had participated in his departure from Gaia. He was gone physically and all evidence of his material existence was also discarded (apart from a few items the boys kept). My experience of being here to undertake these tasks resounded in the painting; leaving the material possessions behind me in the dark shadows, the daily standing at the water's edge of the ocean watching the sunrise also.

Had I manifested this experience through my art? Had Bob and my souls corresponded the same way we had when we'd first met and somehow negotiated a dual response to both of our current spiritual needs? Just as we had written letters unknowingly to each other at the same time in 1975, hatching the idea of travelling the coast of Australia - when we began our lives together.

Questions, always questions ....

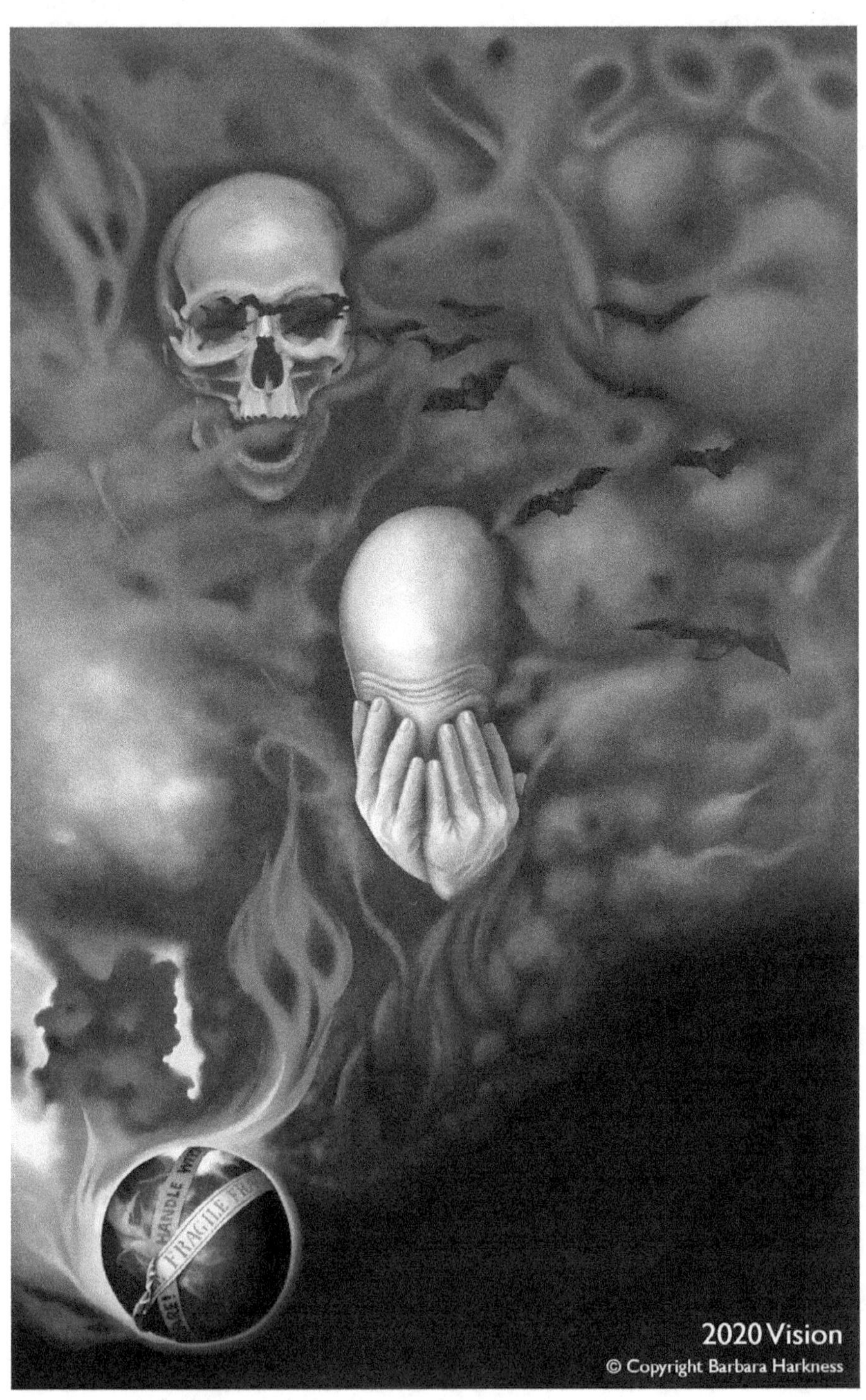

2020 Vision

Chapter 17

2020 - 'unprecedented' challenges

"No great artist ever sees things as they really are.
If he did, he would cease to be an artist"

- Oscar Wilde

Xmas 2019 was spent with my youngest son Max, in Sydney. Daniel had returned to Canada to work on movies, directly after Bob died. It was the best Xmas I'd had in a long time. Not one for all the commercialism and tinsel waste that accompanies the tradition, we booked a counter lunch at the local deli. We dined on oysters, fresh leg ham, and roast Porchetta with crackling on a bed of cauliflower puree. We exchanged cards with words of gratitude from and to each other, in acknowledgement of what had passed that year.

From Sydney, we then travelled to Canberra for a fleeting visit (owing to the worsening bush fires) to the National Gallery to view Picasso and Matisse, who had come to town. South Eastern Australia was quite literally hell on earth; as *unprecedented* weather conditions on the driest continent on earth finally responded with the largest climate change catastrophe the world had ever seen. And watch they did, in horror, as hundreds of fires ravaged the countryside and burnt the drought-stricken, tinder-dry, landscape to a crisp.

The generosity from people all over the world was equal to their horror, as movie stars donated stunning amounts of money for the recovery mission. Nicole Kidman, Bette Midler, Pink, Kylie and Danni Minogue all gave generous financial gifts of $500,000. Chris Hemsworth and Sir Elton John donated $1,000,000 each. Corporations got on board, musicians held events and handed over their proceeds, sports stars auctioned their personal items, working and playing for free to raise funds, to help in the only way they could – through generosity. And the world felt the pain of our suffering too. The kind spiritedness and empathy shown to Australia was heartening.

In 2019 the Amazon rainforest wildfires destroyed 2.2 million acres, and the 2020 California wildfires burned 4.4 million acres. The fires of the Australian Black Summer obliterated 59 million acres - kind of puts it into perspective, doesn't it? An *estimated* one billion animals perished and some endangered species may have been driven to extinction. 5,790 buildings were destroyed, (2,700 were family homes), 31 lives were lost, and our air quality (previously once the most pristine) was suddenly recording the worst pollution levels in the world. Mother nature was certainly reacting, and climate change as well and truly in our face and on our plate, to deal with. No one was denying this, as our nation faced the worst catastrophe and mass evacuations since World War II! The army reserves were put to good use to evacuate the stranded folk on holiday from the beaches, and firefighters from around the globe were dispatched to assist our own tired and weary, battle-scarred men and women. Nature is a hard beast to fight! The realisation was sinking in that this was probably just the beginning of how we would face our future if we kept going in the direction we were - profit over planet. How we live our lives needs to be reconsidered, and FAST!

Owing to the air quality in Sydney, we flew back to South Australia to see in the New Year. We were not exempt from the fires at home either, but the air was clearer owing to the size of the ones burning here. Max looked at my new Mark II version of the painting I had taken over a year to complete. I had not been totally happy with my results, even though it was my portal, as a painting I felt I could do better! I'd enrolled in a one-week Master Class with my art guru Anna Platten, in an effort to hone my painting style. Mark II was an underpainting at this stage with only raw umber and burnt sienna defining the content. Max commented that it looked exactly like Australia did right now, with its red skies ablaze. This gave us inspiration for a painting, which we discussed in great detail. The idea needed a large canvas for impact.

Many artists, Michelangelo, Monet, Picasso included, have destroyed their artwork at some stage of their careers. Baldessari took all of his artwork to a crematorium and reduced everything he had done from 1953 - 1966 to ashes, to make way for a *new style.* In the process of making a valuable documentary of the process: he titled it *'Cremation Project'*, which of course became a work of art in itself. I understand the reasons why an artist would want to destroy something they felt was not quite up to par, especially if it did not meet the artist's expectations. Monet's reasoning for destroying his work was not wanting to devalue his brand.

2020 was the start of a new decade and we both needed a fresh new beginning. This was going to be a collaboration between Max's idea and my painting skills. He had, after all, taken on my business seven years ago, and made it his own. In doing so he had reinvigorated the company with a new name, Co-Partnership; named so on the basis that they work in a team environment with their clients, collaborating on projects. The revised company structure coordinated all aspects of the design process; from strategic research and product analysis, right through to the creation of new brands, inclusive of brand stories. So maybe now it was time for me to listen to his ideas and make them my own. I liked the idea so much that in a split second decision I decided to paint over my large painting to start again, with something different this time - which was not about me, but of the world!

I realised that I had no attachment to the painting, which had taken me over a year to complete. What had changed within me, was a feeling of non-attachment to *things*, which is *precisely* what the painting is about, leaving them behind. The painting owed me nothing; in hours, materials, less the cortisone injections I needed in my elbows to reduce the swelling of bursitis – the result of pure elbow grease required to execute such a mammoth painting. As if I wanted to go through such an excercise again, or needed to, what was I thinking! Perhaps this was my masochistic art phase? I painted over it with black gesso in response to the bush fires, to see from the ashes, what would grow?

We are all observers of life; our own and others. We observe apathy, reaction, mediocrity, melodrama, and injustice; you get the picture. My investigations through art were teaching me how to observe not only the visual aspects of the physical world but also how to portray the hidden qualities of humankind. The obliteration of the massive tarot card was not a predetermined act and I do confess to later regretting my actions, but only momentarily. I had gone through that portal, the purpose had been served.

The images in the media of the massive smoke plumes, blood-red skies, fire tornadoes creating extreme weather patterns, did portray hell on earth. It felt as though Armageddon had arrived! I was deeply affected by the bush fires and I wanted to express my response to what was happening in the world through a painting, the very evidential and undeniable effects of climate change.

At the time I started the painting in February 2020, the world entered into the COVID-19 pandemic as a collective community and was commencing an international shutdown.

Whilst the original intention of the emerging painting was to depict mankind's effect on the planet from an environmental perspective, this was enhanced as the months played out and the painting became progressively more complicated. It was an automated response to what was happening in the real world.

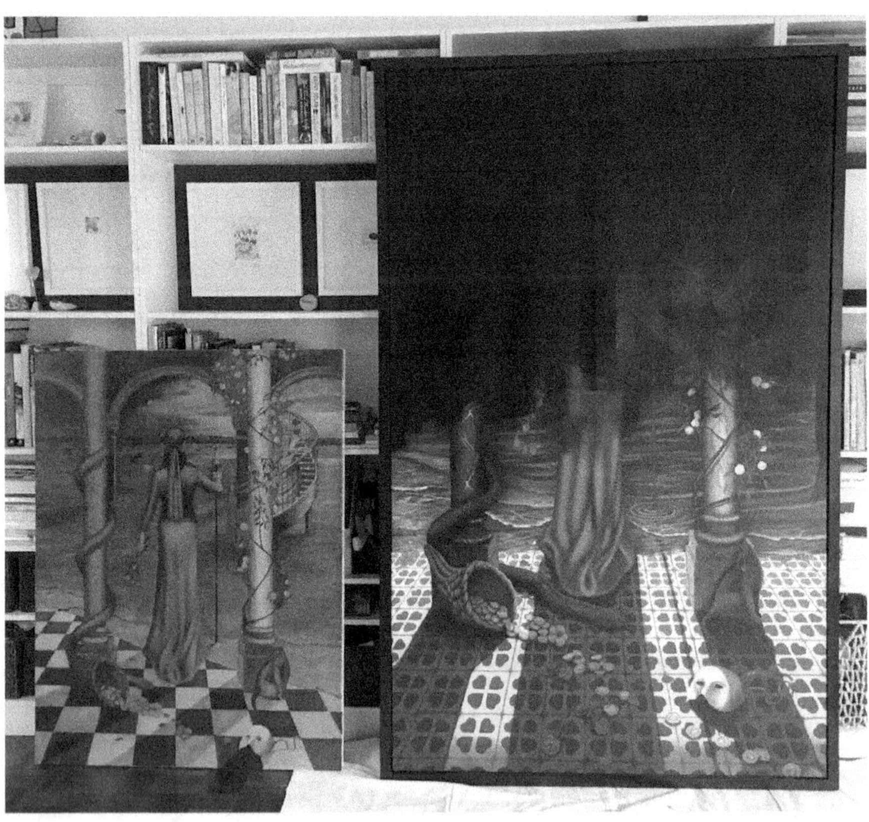

The Magician MkII underpainting The destruction of *The Magician* MkI

Finally, I'd moved past myself! But my oeuvre was still that of *the unseen.* The man covering his eyes in shame - representing mankind's unwillingness to acknowledge the impact we have made upon the earth. Let's not look at the obvious, but suffer the consequences as a result. He is mankind and he is also G.O.D. A catastrophe is unfolding all around and the ramifications of destruction, darkness and death obliterate the whole canvas, whilst a deliberate space of plain black canvas at the bottom right corner represents the nothingness that might remain, should we keep going on this trajectory of man-made destruction.

The Grand Overriding Designer will always step in to show us the lesson we need to learn. This is our fault that Gaia is responding with fire and disease, for we have become too greedy in our consumerism and treatment of Gaia. We had become complacent in our attitudes toward nature. It was only a matter of time before we got the wake-up call.

I worked differently this time, which was automated and without an original sketch, I pulled the idea from my imagination through what I was feeling about the current state of destruction happening globally - both invisible and tangible. As I painted the swirling smoke upon the canvas, ghouls appeared, and so I pulled them out and made them more obvious. By the time COVID 19 had become our worst nightmare, I placed death in the left-hand corner because the painting wasn't looking scary enough, (so my son the art director told me). I can remember feeling very frightened by what felt like a movie about the destruction of the world, and I wondered why we didn't take heed from these very realistic creative movies, which depicted our very worst potential outcomes. Apathy – Greed - Ignorance.

It was the year from hell, and this was how 2020 looked and felt to me. The painting took six months to complete. I pondered the fact that my tarot painting lay beneath the surface and was now invisible, buried beneath 2020 VISION, with its macro-surrealist view of Gaia and humanity's destruction. The lines that had blurred between the seen and unseen were now the same.

Completing the revised painting of *The Magician Mark II,* became my own self-regulated *Honours project.* I had wanted to finish the Arts Degree with an Honours year, however, the Rebel in me decided I didn't need an institutions' grading of assessment, which I knew would make me feel inferior and inadequate. The writing of this book is an adjunct to my painting practice and a personal thesis which has enabled me to fully understand who I am. Writing it all down, exposing myself in words, and painting the pictures, helped me to move past all that I have been, to embrace all that I shall become. Even if that meant unlearning some aspects of whom I had been, for the betterment of who I could, or want to be.

What I have learned and wish to impart through sharing my writing is this:

Be the change that *you* want to be.

Live an authentic life, which reflects your true values.

Be kind to others, and they will respond also with kindness and generosity.

Surrender to the flow of life; it's a glorious feeling when the synchronicity starts and you discover the childlike magic of your youth.

Trust your souls' instincts; because it's always right.

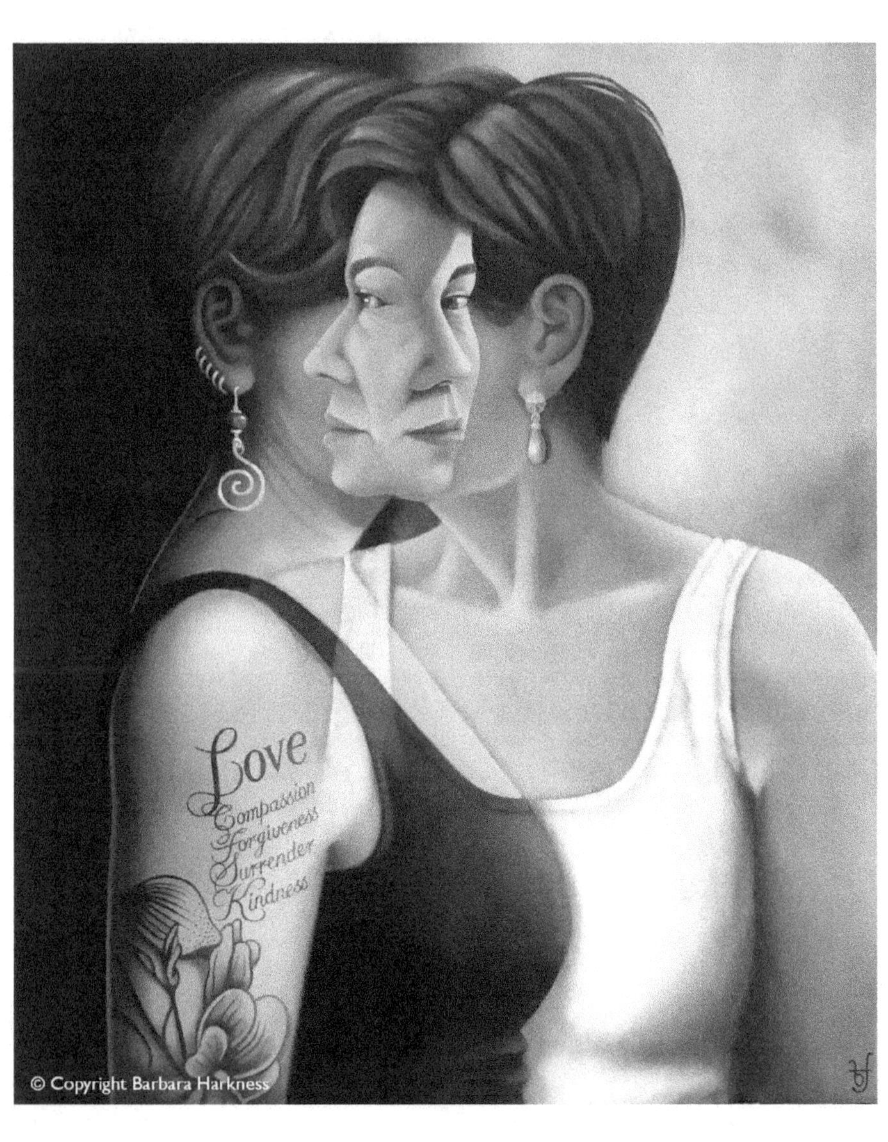

The Divided Self

Chapter 18

Is this the end - or is it the beginning?

We all have our dark side, as well as our light - the yin and yang, the good and bad are aspects of our persona.
Through the steady gaze of the dark persona, a certain harmony is achieved with the light side, which is both disturbing, yet strangely balanced.
The tattoos are an answer to the question of life.
Light will dispel the darkness through acts of compassion, forgiveness, surrender and kindness.
Then love will reign supreme and conquer the darkness in my soul.

- Barbara Harkness

I began the book with the *end* of my second marriage and finished by returning to my first husband - for his *end.* I know that sounds like a riddle. But I do find that there is a certain conundrum about the *end* being a *beginning,* quite simply because that is what happens next. Life is sometimes a riddle you have to work on, to work out! Doors close and others open, just as I embraced the opportunity that had presented itself directly after I finished the painting, and possibly because I knew in my heart that I would have the solitude to create this book. It began in Florence with an unexpected encounter with loneliness. The song about *loneliness* being an *aphrodisiac - truth, beauty and a picture of you -* pretty well sums up the addiction I developed to being alone. These mass of ramblings were written for my cathartic understanding of self. I knew that the *time* I had been given at my husbands home was a *gift* of solitude, which enabled me to pull it all together. I had questioned my life, and taken a journey – this was the journey inside, the one I had experienced as a vision, then painted, which became my reality.

The painting of my giant tarot card I firmly believe was my mortal portal for a very personal transcendence. The physicality of painting such a large picture resulted in bursitis of the elbow, combined with the very human effort of patience and perseverance, which lead me to discover the hidden dimensions of my soul's yearning, by returning to Bob with our sons. I searched for the meaning of spiritualty only to realize that this was a very personal conversation I needed to have with my soul. Through the discovery of human platonic values which are my truth; compassion, harmony, joy, forgiveness, surrender, and of course the most important one – love, my journey and personal legend (according to The Alchemist) was to discover that the most important relationship I would ever have, was the one with myself. By sharing the experience of my journey, it is my hope that *'An affair with my heART'* will show others how easy life can be when you allow yourself to surrender to the flow.

My job here was finally done. I allowed the new owners access to the house to prepare for their new life and caught a plane back to Adelaide and my lovely home. I spent the weekend unpacking my bags and had one last look at the wedding album before placing it into my enormous wooden trunk of memorabilia. My treasure chest of carefully collated memories houses the photo albums, significant birthday cards, the boy's homemade Mothers Day cards, and special letters from dear friends.

The house had been untouched for three months, which made for unlimited days getting it back into shape. I picked up where I left off at Bob's place, by unpacking my own life. I had too much stuff, so I continued with sifting through, selling down, and throwing out!

During the time alone in his house, I'd had a few *spooky* incidents, which I was just bemused by, however, his communication did not stop even in my own home (which we never shared). Strangely, it was here in my own home that I had the clearest communications of all.

He was good at the call and response thing! One morning I had been ruminating about marriage, and whether I felt the need to do this again. This thought of course encapsulated reflection on my second marriage, and our elopement to Italy, where we had planned to marry in Venice but ended up doing this in the small town of Castel Franco instead. Remember, I had not wanted to marry! However, something in me had shifted after returning from caring for Bob. I found the stirrings and a yearning to be in a relationship. Whilst I was happy to be single, I still desired the comfort a good partnership provides, whether it be marriage or simply companionship.

In the guest room, I was in the process of making up the bed with new sheets, when I heard a musical noise ring out. Was it the doorbell or my phone alarm? As I turned in surprise I realised the guitar in the corner of the room had expelled the pick and the notes rang out as if a ghost had quite surely strummed it. To top it off the photograph of Venice on the wall next to the guitar was now hanging at a markedly crooked angle. I couldn't help but smile to myself at the acknowledgement back from him, of my inner thoughts on marriage.

He was here with me, and communicating as any normal spirit force would - or perhaps that shift had occurred in me and I was communicating with him? The incidents mostly involved sound, naturally, because these are vibrational forces. I know that songs can remind us of people, but this next incident was just off the scales - literally; I was driving along in my car and a song by One Republic was playing on the radio. The volume kept involuntarily creeping up and up until the lyrics hit me *'and if we only die once, I wanna die with you,'* on full bore and stayed at that pitch, until I turned it down of course. I had this feeling that he was saying thank you.

The guest room was the scene of another *spooky* encounter - perhaps he was being polite by using the guestroom for these communications? Since I had not lived in the house for three whole months, it needed a good spring clean. Every window, inside and out, was washed, the skirting boards got wiped, chipped doors painted, the leaking roof repaired and ceiling patched below, outdoor umbrellas stitched to repair their hems, plants and hedges clipped. It felt good to give my home a great big cathartic cleanup. I was redesigning the guest room with a minor makeover, which involved removing wallpaper from a wall and repainting it. During the replacement of the furniture, I looked under the bed and noticed that it was particularly dusty. I saw a shiny object, thinking it must be a coin of some denomination, only to be surprised by collecting in with the dust, a plain silver ring. I put the ring on my wedding finger. It fit perfectly. And then I realised the date. It was November 22nd, our wedding anniversary - 44 years ago Bob and I had married on this day! I asked my sons whether they owned the ring, as they were the only ones who had slept in the room, but neither took ownership of it.

Now for some bizarre reason, I could not feel the ring on my wedding finger. I have never been one for wearing rings or bracelets - they seem to annoy me - so I was very happy to not wear these encumbrances of ownership and physical annoyance on my being. This ring was different - I had to check often to see if it was there, owing to its comfort factor, and I mean that in more than the literal sense. I felt Bob's presence with me often, and so I chose to wear the ring, and on my wedding finger! It has become *my Magic ring, the Burden, the Precious, the One,* and I wear it for what it represents to me, for both my marriages, for the love I gave and forgot to give, and to honour the simple gift of life. However, my life now belonged wholly and truly to just *me*, and so I wore it as my *good luck and magic charm*, because that's what it represented, having found it on that meaningful day.

It also occurred to me that Bob had completed his promise too. We had borrowed money to start our life together, therefore I had chosen a really simple ring, which had cost only $10. He'd promised to buy me a *proper* wedding ring when we were more financial. But it never happened, until quite possibly now!

That was the most evidential sign I had from him, but I wondered whether wearing a ring on my wedding finger was the right thing to do if I wanted to meet another partner. It was as if he was in my head and could hear my thoughts. This call and response of spooky happenings always came out of the blue. It had now been 20 months since he'd left, and as time passed the connection seemed to also thin somewhat. Well, that's what I thought! The following morning after *thinking* it might be time to take the ring off, I woke to find it was no longer on my finger, and a search of my jewellery boxes and the location of its origin (under the bed) also came up empty. He was still communicating with me - because what happened next absolutely astounded me. I was revisiting (editing) this part of the book and had read the part about how I felt the ring was my own *magic* ring - my *good luck and magic charm.* That very same day when I found the ring gone, it quite mysteriously fell out of my shopping bag upon unloading the groceries onto the kitchen bench. This was not from my handbag, but a recyclable shopping bag I kept in the back of the car, and I had just packed the bag myself at the supermarket and not noticed it then. It was *not* at the bottom of the bag, but fell out as if it was placed on the top (of the sweet potatoes to be precise) and tumbled to the floor with a very loud toss and spin - just like a magic trick!

When I did some exterior renovations to my property, a solid brick wall was demolished to make way for a brand new Corten steel wall, complete with a new gate. There was an intercom system in the old wall, which had been demolished, but the phone remained on the hallway wall inside the house (a removal job for an electrician at a later date). There was no doorbell to ring, the device had been well and truly demolished along with the wall and the wires had all been cordoned off. However, the doorbell kept ringing on odd occasions. I would pick up the phone and half expected Bob to be on the other end! I had to disconnect the phone as well owing to it becoming a regular (and annoying) event. The spooky thing which happened afterwards (and confirmation that this was indeed *very spooky*) was when the new doorbell installation (which was just a buzzer) rung in the early hours one morning and was not my designated chime! A wireless device, which had multiples of tones to select from, I chose the regular *ding-dong*, over the *barking dog* or choices of other cheesy tunes. However, what buzzed and woke me was the chime *banjo on my knee*. That morning I checked the doorbell and found that my *ding-dong* choice was still active. Was the banjo chime simply another message of contact? You see, Bob's father played the banjo, and one of the treasured items from Bob's estate of memorabilia was the broken long arm of his father's banjo. It was quite a beautiful piece of art with an inlaid mother of pearl and ivory. The banjo chimed again in the early hours of the morning when Max came to stay. I asked if he heard it, and he had.

My conclusion about the after-life is my own belief and I entertain the idea that when we die, the energy and intelligent consciousness we once were becomes the air we breathe. Hence the reference to *The Universe*, the all-encompassing mass that we are, which connects us all to the earth, to animals, to the elements that are the air, to the water which sustains us, to the sun which warms us, the plants which nurture us, and to each other, the Collective Unconscious (Carl Jung) and the Conscious

Collective (ultra-connected invisible world-wide-web) and the soul of the world (Paul Coelho's Alchemist).

I entertain the idea of reincarnation because being human is a fantastic feeling and I want it to go on and on forever, but I would rather find a newer body than live in this one, which will eventually betray me. I am not trying to enforce my findings, just exposing what I have experienced as my truth by sharing my stories. I like to see the unseen in my world, to feel the presence of those no longer present, and trust in the unknown because I do know that there is more to my existence than my physical body.

This task I undertook; the act of compassion in helping Bob in his final weeks on Gaia was life-transforming for me. Somehow the act of giving, and I mean truly giving of myself, not just superficially being present, must have been a first for me. Because the love I felt during the act of caring for my family once more during such an important time, made me understand what love was. Love is quite simply the giving of oneself. It is not something, which is extracted from another. It lives within us all, and the acts of kindness, compassion, forgiveness and surrender are all you need to access *love*.

I know that I have left myself open for criticism through my analytical exposure, especially in my search for love. This is my confession; I found the love inside which enabled me to write about the human condition from my experiences. I know I am not that different to other women either. Writing about my father, and lack of love for him, I hope will show others – especially men - that it is important to love your daughters so that they grow into fully loving women who search for love in a potential mate through their relationship with you as an example of what a good relationship looks like. This is where love starts, with the family, by showing our children how to love. Just writing about this has made me understand myself as a consequence.

Love your neighbours and your friends, as this reverses hate. In a world where we have these polarising attitudes and there are so many kinds of love, and of course, the one we all associate with and yearn for in that one word is *romantic* love. My search led me back to the start, to my first true love. But it was not anything like the romantic love we had when we first met. It was the act of compassion, which opened the door, a very interior door. It was the door to my own heart. The act of caring, and showing my children that we (Bob and I) still cared, filled me with love, and made me feel complete. Perhaps it was the selflessness of it, or quite simply the act of kindness, which gave me the courage to say that I was a better person as a result.

I have always known that it is a fallow search to look for someone to complete you, to fill in the gaps where you are not. Perhaps loving generates more love, and the more you show, the more you fill up your own cup. Romantic love wears off, and it's what's left that requires the attention to continue generating the love machine, from both parties. If the balance gets out of kilter, that's when the cups get drained. Discussion, communication, appreciation are all that are required for a successful loving relationship between two people. It's not difficult, but then it can also be as difficult as we want it to be, through our stupid human faults - or our magnificent benevolent human qualities.

The dualities that make us human, good - bad, mean – kind, selfish – selfless, giving – taking, loud – quiet, - what sort of human do you want to be?

It is always a *choice*.

What a privilege it is to be human, and to experience this

wonderful existence we have on such a beautiful planet, with so much diversity for our exploration. T.S. Elliot put it so eloquently; *'and I shall not cease from exploring, if only to find myself back at the beginning, and recognise the place for the very first time.'* I believe that sometimes we *recognise* the place or a person and so, therefore, it or they, feel very familiar to us. And the journey begins once more.

Chapter 19

This is my Renaissance

Once a wise man was asked…
"what is the meaning of life?"
He replied…"Life itself has no meaning,
life is an opportunity to create a meaning."
–Wise Man

The Magician painting was a questioning: a knock on the door to my inner life. *What is this all about?* We question our purpose in being here, seeking it, finding it, a highly personal and individual everlasting search in our own never-ending story. A personal *Mission Impossible*, should you accept the challenge to discover what your forte in life is!

After I had finished the 2020 Vision painting I returned to finally finish the painting of Goddess Tyche, myself in the dream, the Magician from the tarot. The painting could mean anything I wanted it to. Or it could be interpreted as my friend, Milica, had read it, via her intuitive process, which was pretty spot on. That is the beauty of art, the viewer makes his or her summary of the work, and it may strike a chord, which reads differently from my actual intention.

But what of the grander picture? This was the question art was asking of me. I had built so much in my material world, but what of the inner world of psyche, soul and life thereafter? I had reached a level of comfort, which told me I didn't need any more than I have. I also had enough money to survive the remainder of my days - if I didn't go nuts with it, that is.

So my reader, having come to the end of my book, I feel that I do owe you a written explanation of the painting. Of course, the entire book is the justification of my journey - the Fool's journey, the Magician's power, the Goddess within, and finding my truth.

For the uninitiated, a little info on the symbolism in painting from the Renaissance art period. The deeper you delve into Renaissance art, the more intriguing and open to interpretation it becomes. The Renaissance period (14th-17th centuries) was one of the longest in art history and encompassed changing human ideals in the natural world. The Renaissance was a fervent period of European cultural, artistic, political and economic rebirth, following the middle ages and generally promoted the rediscovery of classical philosophy, literature and art.

Nearly all art was created through commissions, either from the church or the extremely wealthy and powerful Medici family. Therefore the themes were nearly always religious and the stories were usually depictions of heaven or hell. Keep in mind that the masses at this time were largely illiterate and so the paintings were a powerful way to keep the common folk in check. Certain items and colours became a code for meaning and created an insightful visual language. There are symbols that have consistency in their meaning and make recurrent appearances in prominent masterpieces. Towards the high Renaissance, Religion became a less common theme and the humanities made their way onto the canvas and told less *severe* stories.

Colours: Reds always meant high social status, orange was worn by middle-ranked people, yellows depicted prostitutes, green symbolised youth, love and joy, light blue was for women of marriageable age, white for purity, browns were for religious dressings, grey for peasants, purple was again a rich colour as it was popularized by the Medici family, which wore Purple. The colour and use of flowers; a carnation in Greek means *flower of god,* therefore a red carnation or rose symbolised love, a pink carnation is a symbol of marriage, a cornflower was the enemy of snake, in particular, a blue cornflower represented heaven, and an iris symbolizes a divine message and trust.

Animals: A serpent always indicated something evil or satanic, and the opposite of this is a dove, which implied reference to the Holy Spirit. A swan signified purity.

Food also had great symbolic significance; pomegranates mean desire, fertility and marriage, but can also mean resurrection and immortality in certain cases. An apple is synonymous with evil - we instantly reference damned Eve for her part in the downfall from the grace of mankind. Pear is for incarnation, a gourd implies the resurrection and of course, grapes are the symbol of Bacchus, the god of wine.

My personal symbology is as follows: I stand between two solid marble pillars, which create a dichotomy; forces of dark and light, shedding and growth, evil and good, masculine and feminine, night and day. These also represent the material world, as does the floor with the discarded, unnecessary remnants of my life now well and truly in the past. The cornucopia of spilling coins on the left-hand side of the painting is my readiness to let go of materiality, in preference for spirituality. The white mask means I no longer feel the need to be something I am not, nor willing to hide my real self. The cat in front of the right pillar is, quite simply, my Scottish good luck charm looking out for me. These items are the same and have not changed from the original painting.

Blindfolded, I hold my candle staff for support, light and guidance; this is my craft and forte, the gift of art. The snake on the dark pillar is the dark side, and he (the masculine) represents the shedding. The white rose vine of the right light pillar (the feminine) is my growth and is indicative of new life. Before me is a wall with archways. Beyond the architectural aspect and in spiritual terms, archways represent transitioning from one place to another. The symbolism of the arch is the division between the secular world of man and the sacred world of the Ancients. Thus the arch allows those who have earned the right to proceed into the presence of the sublime and the spiritual. As an archetypal symbol, the archway is fundamentally masculine. In mythology, arches & doorways are understood as thresholds in time and space (Chronos/ physical world) through which one passes to enter another kind of time and space (kairos/spiritual world). In tarot, most archways on the cards are fitted with pillars, which convey a sense of duality. The duality of the pillars works with the archway meaning, because often we're faced with some kind of contrast that prompts us to shift, and move through the archway to a new perspective, or revived life. The sea in spiritual terms represents birth, love, death and resurrection. In the natural world, the ocean is a symbol of power, strength, life and mystery; its changeability and unpredictable nature set us at its mercy. In dreams, the ocean may represent a bridge between the conscious and unconscious mind. A calm ocean may indicate a feeling of peace and tranquillity, whereas a violent ocean may indicate a resistance toward the connection between minds. In psychology, the ocean is a symbol for the mother. It may bring the dreamer back to a time when they were taken care of. The ocean is the origin of all life forms, and so the ocean also symbolises life.

As I stand on this precipice between the natural and the spiritual world, with my trusted magician wand firmly placed in the water ready to embark upon my journey, I am reminded of the statement, *'As above-so below'*. The term means that what is bound in heaven will also be found on Earth. I refer to this in a religious context, as I believe this is where the text comes from. In modern terms, this also refers to the mind and soul: the world outside *(above)* the individual *is* the natural world, and inside *(below)* the spiritual world where the soul resides. Together, the intent of the phrase is to remind the magic practitioner that they cannot achieve their purpose without first achieving harmony between spiritual and physical. That phrase is believed to be the key to all magic. It means that what is within me is also outside of me. As it is on earth, so it is in heaven. As I am, so are my cells, so are my atoms, and so is G.O.D. (Grand Overriding Designer – ME!)

In the Mark II version, I changed three major aspects; the location of the sun, and the sky, which depicts both night and day. The sun appears twice. It is rising in the middle, therefore creating an orange glow, and then again at the early stage of the day placed to the right, which casts shadows across the painting at angles to suggest the movement of my invisible, inner world. The shadows are leaving the canvas, and it is clear that the left side where darkness resides is becoming less involved, and the right side brighter and fuller.

At the stairwell I have removed my blindfold, hence indicating an enlightenment process has happened upon my journey, and I can now understand my inner world, that of the soul. Or perhaps this is my preparedness to see more clearly? The inner world I had searched for was now being revealed in the natural world. The journey back to Bob was my personal road of discovery. I realised that confronting my demons, to right the wrongs I have done to others, is the first step on the road to compassion. This door can only be enabled through the generosity of spirit, of surrender, kindness and compassion, which fills you so completely. These are not material things; they are invisible. They will fulfil and override any other human desire.

I placed a golden egg in the foreground corner. Whilst this may have the appearance of being in my past, it references a time when I knew how to attract money. It's the Phoenix egg awaiting her re-birth into the world again.

Interestingly, I made these changes on the right-hand side of the painting, as if reading a page from left to right, there is no-where else to go after mark II of the painting, but I'm sure there will be a response to it. Symbolically, there is a reference to being closer to G.O.D, as it's a well-known fact that the Renaissance painters would place the *Godly* folk on the right-hand side of Him, and the riffraff on the left. These aspects of the painting weren't analysed till after I'd made the adjustments. But I was pleased that I was making progress in the right direction, by following my heART.

My most creative time of the day is when I first wake. The dawn of every new day is a source of inspiration, yet the past reflects into my pool of knowledge ... and I love this for all my life experiences and how they inform me. I am grateful in this current troubled world that my inner world is a safe place, my very own sanctuary. And this is why I paint. I am processing the past, arriving (always arriving), yet positively excited for the future.

One morning I woke with the song in my head, *Losing my Religion*, by R.E.M. A quick Google search revealed the perfect words to match my painting. I considered re-naming the painting for the third time. But decided against it. I liked the tarot aspect, the magic I had created through painting it. *The Magician*, was here to stay.

I also usually write first thing in the morning, on a *reMarkable* tablet, which converts the writing to text, which I then edit into the book at my computer later in the day (usually after a couple of hours of painting). That morning when I sat down to do my writing in my favourite corner of the room, on a bean bag next to the open French doors, a car pulled up outside with the radio blaring, and guess what song was playing? Yep, you guessed it, *Losing my Religion*, and they obviously liked it too because it played till the very end, and then they turned the radio off and left. You know, I never went outside to check up to see if it was indeed coming from a car radio, I just loved the little synchronistic incidents, which came along to endorse my beliefs. It affirmed that it was my song for the book. I like to put music to my writing, and therefore connect with another artist, which is what art is, a communal connection and way of sharing between us all. For me, *Losing my Religion* was not about *religion*, but rather the dissolution of old beliefs, outdated societal ideals, and the masks we wear to accommodate the archetypal roles we play. R.E.M. guitarist Peter Buck wrote the main riff and chorus to the song and singer Michael Stipe's vocals were recorded in a single take. Stipe has repeatedly stated that the song's lyrics are not about religion. The phrase *Losing my Religion* is simply a romantic expression of feeling frustrated and desperate by unrequited love.

Stipe says, "It's just a classic obsession pop song, and I've always felt the best kinds of songs are the ones where anybody can listen to it, put themselves in it and say "Yeah, that's me" just as art does.

That's me in the corner
That's me in the spot-light, losing my religion
What if all these fantasies come flailing around
…and now I've said too much
I thought that I heard you laughing
I thought that I heard you sing
I think I thought I saw you try
But that was just a dream
And that's *LIFE IMITATING ART!*

Epilogue

"When we have the courage to walk into our story and own it, we also get to write the ending"

- Brene Brown

The process of self-discovery, enlightenment, call it what you will, is a highly personal journey. I share my journey in the hope that it will inspire others to attain the wonder of living in the pure moment, and how to live a creative and responsible existence. Many people have inspired me and continue to do so. The writer who inspired me to write this book was Liz Gilbert. Renown for her bestseller *Eat Pray Love*, I loved her book *Big Magic* too, which is about just that; creating Magic in your life. I thought it was a brave title, Magic? Mmmm! But whilst we are on that subject, what about Manifesting, and Meditation. G.O.D only knows that we have manifested a mess with our presence here on Gaia. Besides, most manifesting stories I have read or watched all seemed to be about manifesting more money, cars, or bigger houses into existence. It also felt like a buzzword of the decade that just got bandied around, *alot!*

Therefore I wasn't into Manifesting.

I liked the idea of Meditation – but to be honest, I found the act of meditation to be quite tricky. I think I know how it feels because I've often just found myself zoned out, and simply not thinking of anything at all. La La Land! It happens when I'm deeply relaxed, sometimes even whilst listening to others talk. I know that sounds rude, doesn't it? I go to this zone when I paint. However, meditation still fascinates me, owing to the fact I can't seem to *get there* when I deliberately try. I also find it difficult to sit bolt upright, which is not comfortable, or conducive to feeling fully relaxed, and therefore it's highly probable that it won't happen!

I did however enjoy the process of creative visualisation when I studied the Akashics and so this was my own take on how to start my day in the creative realm. I'm an early waker, often around 4 am. But I don't like to get up when it's dark. I also love my bed and snuggling down into a state of luxurious human comfort. During these early hours and in a semi slumber, I would visualise walking along the pathway to the beach at Casuarina, specifically to watch the sunrise. I was there, rather than in my bed. On the beach were three children, around age five, my two sons and myself as a child. They would run to greet me, hugging my legs, full of joy to see me. Younger Barbara would remain in the distance, and I would have to go to her and initiate a hug. She was wearing my favourite dress, which my grandmother had made for me. Young Barbara did not smile very much, she was reserved, shy almost. I hardly recognised her. Slowly, day-by-day I would bring her into my family fold with the boys and we'd build sandcastles together. Then finally one morning when I arrived at the beach she was already with them, playing and building sandcastles.

Then Bob started to appear in my morning visualisations.

Now I didn't intend to include him, he just gatecrashed the party because he wanted in! There must have been a reason, and so I let him in. He would walk to the scene from the waves (which is where we left him two years prior) and be around 40 years old. Superfit, very handsome Bob - in his budgie smugglers I might add! Now the clothes were an interesting aspect because I didn't seem to have any control over how the players on my stage were dressed. The only person whose clothes I cannot articulate at all are my own, (excluding my younger and older selves) and I figured that must be because I am the observer. My two sons always wore simple shorts and T-shirts; beachwear from Target (they'll hate me putting that in)!

Bob and I never hugged, but there was a really strong acknowledgement that he missed us all. I started to enjoy seeing him in my entourage. On subsequent visits, he would go straight to the children and play with them.

"Daddy, daddy", they would scream in delight when they saw him.

He asked me who the little girl was one time. "Oh that's me", I replied.

He just smiled back at me, of course. She was also the little girl we never had. I think Bob had also longed for a daughter to complete our family.

On my exit from the beach, I would visit my older self, who sat on the bench seat overlooking the scene playing out before her and the magnificent backdrop of Casuarina beach. Again, I had no control over her attire or how she looked - but my older self was also my higher self. Dressed in flowing white robes, my hair was bright white like my mother's had been. It was with her that I would have my deep and meaningful early morning conversation, asking for clarification on my life's direction. And then I would exit the beach.

One morning I decided to meet with just Bob for a talk on the bench seat, without my older self. We watched the children playing and sat side by side. I didn't start the conversation this time, he did. He said he was sorry for not acknowledging me more, or listening to what my needs were. He realised the mistakes he had made as well and wanted to let me know he now knew where *he* went wrong with the marriage. We touched hands and looked into each other's eyes in acceptance.

Now here's the *spooky* part. The second anniversary of Bob's passing was approaching. I got a text from Max saying that he wanted to go to Casuarina for a commemorative visit, and asked if I wanted to join him. I said I'd love to, of course.

Then Daniel was offered a job in Byron Bay, which is a 20-minute drive to Casuarina. He had been living and working in Canada since Bob's passing and was suffering from the northern hemisphere lock-down restrictions. Owing to everything pleasurable being shut, the only option was to work. The post-production movie companies never closed up shop, in fact they were busier than ever with the ever-increasing demand for home viewing platforms content. Australia was booming on the back of Covid-mania, and reversed attitudes to living a good life on home soil meant many ex-pats were coming back to roost. It was an attractive and safe place to live, always had been, but Covid made us superstars in the world arena of desirable and sustainable living.

Now here's the *really spooky* part: Daniel's job contract start date was May 2nd - the anniversary of Bob's death. I organised the accommodation for us in Byron Bay, and for some bizarre reason, I put four people into the search engine and didn't realise my *subconscious* mistake until well afterwards. We got an upgrade to a superior beach house when I missed out on the more affordable option. Someone was looking out for us!

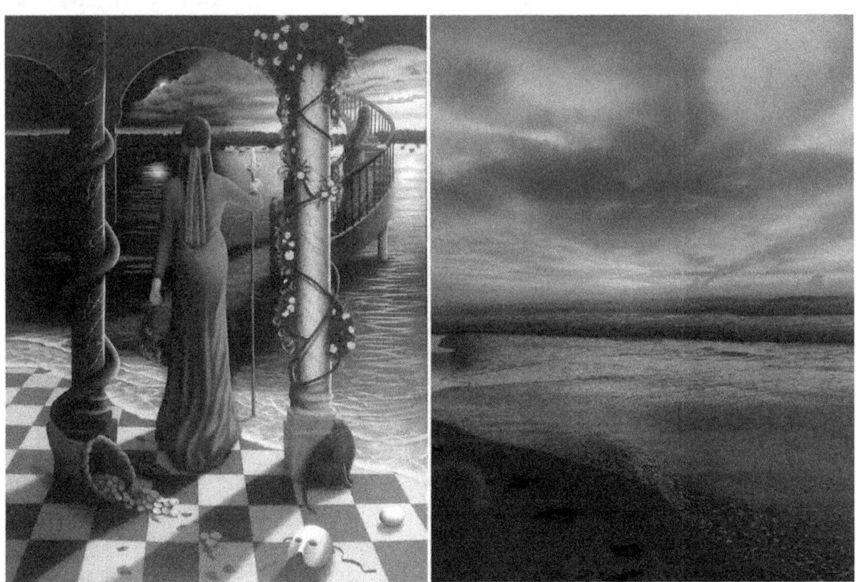

The week was indeed magic. I had not seen Daniel in two years and so it was a very special reunion on many levels. Every morning without fail we went down to the beach to watch the sunrise, even though this was initially met with resistance! The weather was mildly inclement with scattered rain throughout the week, therefore the clouds always provided a magnificent display. On the last day of the holiday when we ventured down to the beach for our last sunrise, I could see the sky ablaze from the house and just knew that we were in for a spectacular surprise. And it was - a show of all shows. A sky like no other I had ever seen - it was literally on fire! Appearing more like a sunset, blazing in colours of vivid orange and cadmium red. I could not help but notice that there were two bulbous clouds on the horizon, which caused two shadows from the rising sun to reflect all the way across and up to the top of the sky – in fact they reflected at the same angle of the shadows in my painting! This synchronistic sign from the natural world, signalling to me, gave me such joy. A wink from the Grand Overriding Designer to affirm that I was indeed on the right path, that life *could* follow art and vice versa. It was all the confirmation I needed to know that I had tapped into the thread of all consciousness - the soul of the world - call it what you wish. I understood that life is a rich tapestry and that we weave our own pictures. The older we get - the richer the tapestry. I had also come to a deeper understanding that life's cycles, patterns and lessons repeatedly teach us how to live a good life, and with the privilege of age comes the wisdom that flows from these teachings. I also discovered that endings were in fact beginnings, and at the sunset of my life - I found my sunrise.

"Viva la Vida" (Love live life)

– Frida Kahlo

"Art washes away from the soul the dust of everyday life."

- Pablo Picasso

"The emotions are sometimes so strong that I work without knowing it. The strokes come like speech."

- Vincent van Gogh

"The object of art is not to reproduce reality, but to create a reality of the same intensity."

- Alberto Giacometti

"An artist is not paid for his labor but for his vision."

- James McNeill Whistler

"The position of the artist is humble. He is essentially a channel."

- Piet Mondrian

"Painting is the grandchild of nature. It is related to God."

- Rembrandt

"Life IS *Art"*

- Barbara Harkness

INDEX OF PAINTINGS

Acknowledgments

There are so many people who inspire me; sages, prophets and artists, the living and the passed, their gifts continue on. Whilst I painted in the studio I would listen while Deepak Chopra, Oprah Winfrey, Gregg Braden, Joe Dispenza, Caroline Myss, Stuart Wilde, Elizabeth Gilbert, Michael Singer, Brene Brown, dispensed their wisdom. Artists who have influenced my work; Anna Platten, Pablo Picasso, Jackson Pollock, Vincent van Gogh, Alberto Giacometti, James McNeill Whistler, Piet Mondrian, Rembrandt, Leonardo Da Vinci, Salvador Dali, John Baldessari. Philosophers and writers whose quotes and passages I have used: Carl Jung (much of this book has been based upon his theories, so he gets the biggest THANK-YOU), Paul Coelho, Michael Beckwith, Robert Fritz, Caroline Myss, Brene Brown, William Butler Yeats, Shonda Rhimes (TV producer), A.A Milne, T.S. Elliot, Blaise Pascal, Aesop, Francis of Assisi, Lois McMaster Bujold (author) Sai Baba, Ghandi, Oscar Wilde, Loretta Young (singer). Songwriters whose words I have also referenced; Peter Buck and Michael Stipe (Losing my Religion), Richard Lee Wold and Tony George Colton (I remember LA). Movie stars I have mentioned throughout the book; Jane Fonda, Nicole Kidman, Bette Midler, Pink, Kylie & Danni Minogue, Chris Hemsworth, Sir Elton John, & Kelly Slater. A special thank-you to my sons Daniel and Max, for simply being in my life - I'm glad we all chose each other. My best friend since 1974 - Eileen Williams: we both arrived in Australia from foreign shores and became first flat mates and then soul sisters for life. I definitely chose her over the flat, liked her straight away! We have known each other's darkest secrets for well on 47 years now - therefore she held my reputation in the highest degree when deciphering what needed to be deleted from my ramblings. She has also been extremely encouraging of my creative endeavors. My sister Linda for her grammatical editing, she always looked after all of us – it was her role, thank-you. I have gone over this manuscript so many times I have lost count, and so if there are still a few typos or grammatical errors, please excuse - apparently perfection is impossible (according to Salvador Dali). Others I have mentioned in the book who gave their time; Milica Bilandzic Popovic for her intuitive analysis of the Magician painting. Majken, Paul, Charlize and Sophia Fussek - the family who purchased Bob's house and became friends. It has been my hope that my story will also inspire others, which is my soul reason for releasing this highly personal memoir.

Permissions: I acknowledge that I was given permission to use excerpts from the following authors: Robert Fritz. Caroline Myss; Hay House Inc., copyright 2013. Carlsbad CA. Anna Platten, personal permission has been granted.

Quotes: I have tried to obtain permission from all those living for the use of their words or quotes, however this process is not always achievable through search channels. And so I apologise if my message did not get through, and hope that you are OK with my referencing your wisdom or your poetry of words from songs. I am led to believe that using less than 600 words is OK, but I am new at this; my intention was not appropriation, rather the sharing of your wisdom and so I hope you are OK with that. In fact many of these excerpts were referenced through Instagram as spoken words.

We are all one.

www.ingramcontent.com/pod-product-compliance
Lightning Source LLC
LaVergne TN
LVHW050622100826
845148LV00011B/1701

* 9 7 8 0 6 4 5 6 7 1 2 0 9 *